Advanced Praise for
Hands Off! The Disappearance of Touch in the Care of Children

"In this work, Richard Johnson explores the hysteria about 'no touch' policies in early childhood education in the United States and Australia. Through theoretical analysis and through the voices of teachers he deftly illustrates the manufactured moral panic that has turned the everyday relational lives of teachers and young children upside down, and he explores the shifting discourses about sexuality, desire, and children's bodies, which appear to be paving the way for a rigid Victorian morality in early childhood centers—a morality that is replacing old-fashioned concerns about attachment, caring, love, and affection with a highly technologized concept of caregiving, buttressed by pervasive electronic surveillance. This book raises troubling questions for any reader interested in the psychic welfare of children."

Michael O'Loughlin, Hofstra University

"Richard Johnson challenges a growing orthodox·· ᴉth worrying and damaging to children's emotional hᴇ· n whatever settings, demand and need contaᴄᵗ is part of this expectation. Professionᴀ ᴉcational settings, especially men, will fiᵢ .nallenging, supportive and questioning. Abo .ne tide of political correctness that wishes to take ovᴇ .care field."

Brian Cheeseman, Principal Lecturer in Playwork Studies,
Leeds Metropolitan University

Hands Off!

Eruptions
New Thinking across the Disciplines

Erica McWilliam
General Editor

Vol. 2

PETER LANG
New York • Washington, D.C./Baltimore • Boston • Bern
Frankfurt am Main • Berlin • Brussels • Vienna • Canterbury

Richard T. Johnson, 1956-

Hands Off!

The Disappearance of Touch in the Care of Children

PETER LANG

New York • Washington, D.C./Baltimore • Boston • Bern
Frankfurt am Main • Berlin • Brussels • Vienna • Canterbury

Library of Congress Cataloging-in-Publication Data

Johnson, Richard T.
Hands off! : the disappearance of touch in the care of children / Richard T. Johnson.
p. cm. — (Eruptions; vol. 2)
1. Teacher-student relationships. 2. Early childhood education—Social aspects.
3. Child care—Social aspects. 4. Child sexual abuse—Prevention. I. Title. II. Series.
LB1033.J63   372.1102'3—dc21   98-3317
ISBN 0-8204-3983-5
ISSN 1091-8590

Die Deutsche Bibliothek-CIP-Einheitsaufnahme

Johnson, Richard T.:
Hands off! : the disappearance of touch in the care of children / Richard T. Johnson.
–New York; Washington, D.C./Baltimore; Boston; Bern;
Frankfurt am Main; Berlin; Brussels; Vienna; Canterbury: Lang.
(Eruptions; Vol. 2)
ISBN 0-8204-3983-5

Cover design by Lisa Dillon

The paper in this book meets the guidelines for permanence and durability
of the Committee on Production Guidelines for Book Longevity
of the Council of Library Resources.

© 2000 Peter Lang Publishing, Inc., New York

Printed in the United States of America

To my mother and father who first touched me and to my wife Tina and children Nick, Nathan, and Haleigh, who allow me to touch them and understand better what my parents taught me so many years ago.

Contents

Foreword by Erica McWilliam   ix

Acknowledgments   xvii

Introduction   1

Chapter 1   Touch or "No Touch"   7

Chapter 2   "No Touch" as Moral Panic   17

Chapter 3   Strange Stories of Surveillance   35

Chapter 4   Strange Stories of Desire   51

Chapter 5   The Sexual Dynamics of
             "Touching" Pedagogy   61

Chapter 6   Soothing a Crying Child in the
             Age of "No Touch"   73

Chapter 7   (Re)Claiming Touch   83

Appendix   91

References   97

Index   117

Foreword

Nothing is less certain today than sex, behind the liberation of its discourse. And nothing today is less certain than desire, behind the proliferation of its images.

—Jean Baudrillard, *Seduction*

Never before have we witnessed so much activity dedicated to boundary-riding desire in relation to children. At a time when the proliferation of discourses about sex is unprecedented, we want to be certain that any desire to engage with children is not motivated by sex or productive of sex. Our collective determination to put an end to child sexual victimization—to govern desire in the interests of children—demands the maximum scope for social mechanisms of surveillance, and greater penalties for the abuser. To achieve this, we must leave no aspect of children's lives and relationships unscrutinized, and this includes powerful invitations to produce retrospective readings of our own childhood experiences. Our intentions are noble—caring for the vulnerable is, after all, a hallmark of the progressive society, and who could be more vulnerable than an innocent child?

Thus, all those who come into contact with children—nanny or neighbor, priest or pedagogue—now find themselves with more explicit obligations and responsibilities as nurturers and caregivers. Every child-adult or even child-child relationship has been rendered more scrutinized, more regulated, more governable by a combination of tactics—professional expertise, media reporting, policy proliferation, community organization, legislative reform, and so on.

At the same time that we celebrate the triumph of every new piece of child protection legislation, every nursery observation camera installed, every pedophile convicted and placed behind bars, we are being forced to acknowledge some very troubling implications for anyone in close proximity to a child. As Richard Johnson demonstrates so ably in this book, the means by which we currently identify and eliminate abusive practices are never innocent: they can and do have unintended negative effects. Powerful mechanisms of surveillance and control are ushering in new ideas about *who* is vulnerable and *under what conditions* this vulnerability is likely to manifest itself as a moral or legal problem. Johnson shows this new politics of vulnerability can actually be harmful for some children and for those adults who seek to love them to their ultimate good. Harm results when either adult or child learns to fear the social and legal repercussions of an appropriate and pleasurable adult-child intimacy, such as the pleasures Johnson shares with his own daughter.

Richard Johnson joins Joe Tobin (1997) in providing compelling evidence that professional caregivers are being trained to read adult-child interaction differently for better and worse. They are learning to be more solicitous and more anxious to "see" things that they did not "see" before. The more professional they are, the more anxious they should be. It begins to be impossible for any good citizen to see a father cuddle his daughter in the park, a stranger offer comfort to a young or disabled child, Santa sit Sarah on his knee, without a sense of disquiet or ambivalence. In this precise moment, some body is guilty of suspicion of abuse. But it is not simply the present context that demands such scrutiny—all of us are invited to reflect differently on past events. And so in our wisdom in 1999 at age 40, our uncle's tickles to our bare belly over thirty years ago become available to be reinscribed as pernicious rather than playful.

I have written elsewhere of my own disquiet about this new politics of vulnerability and its effects on teachers. In doing so I have joined a number of feminist writers—Alison Jones, Meaghan Morris, Vicki Kirby, and Jane Gallop—who seek to raise questions about the social production of vulnerability in infantilized "others," such as students and women. As female and feminist writers, it has been easier for all of us to do this work than it is for a person like the author of this book. As a male in a School of Early Childhood, Richard Johnson is more awkwardly located in terms of the child-abuse narrative. While he has the good fortune to be surrounded at the University of Hawaii by colleagues of both sexes who are alert to the tyrannies that moral panics can generate, this is all too rare in early childhood as an area of scholastic endeavor. The attractions of a highly romantic psychologized identity for the "growing and developing"child have unfortunately been more seductive than any appeal to subject this very idea to scrutiny in the interests of actual children and their caregivers. Mainstream early childhood scholarship remains wedded to a particular combination of liberal humanism and child psychology, whose effect on tertiary courses is deodorizing to the point of sterility. The result is a profession in which there is a surfeit of virgin mothers and a dearth of debate.

This is not the only reason, however, that the book Johnson has written is timely and important. The "quality" era of policymaking is not coping well with subtle distinctions of the sort that ought to be made between eros and sex. Eros is too slippery an idea for black-and-white logic, and is all too often collapsed into sex, which, in the context of children, is necessarily abuse. Policy reform which proceeds out of this logic addresses pedagogical work as if eros (pleasure and desire) have nothing to do with understanding. Learning is held to be in essence a cognitive exercise, best done in an atmosphere of supportive care. The result is that present institutional investments in good pedagogy are likely to take the form of "best practice" policy proliferation, performance indicators, and platitudes.

Such activities cannot put an end to the problem of abuse in childcare settings or anywhere else. This is not simply because they are unable to grapple with the ambiguity of *eros* as the *circulation* of power and desire in human relationships within organizations. It is also that these activities themselves proliferate new forms of child abuse, inasmuch as they reinscribe any number of daily practices as potentially abusive under certain circumstances. Just as we have proliferated categories of special learning needs in children (ADD, ADHD, ODD, and so on) to ensure that no individual is unaccounted for, now we are producing more anxiety—and therefore a stronger imperative to self-regulation—about every aspect of our engagement with children, from bathing to breakfast-time. Is our toweling stimulating and thereby abusing their bodies? Should they be allowed to choose their own breakfast cereal? What if their choice is not a medically sanctioned one—is this potentially abusive? And so on.

The caring relationship, like the pedagogical relationship, is ambiguous and duplicitous, because it is produced out of desire. Moves to separate the "good/ethical/unsex" bits of desire from the "bad/unethical/sex" bits of desire cannot help but misrecognize the nature of eros in the caregiving relationship. In the rush to end abuse, we have waged war on eros, with the result that one set of tyrannies has given way to another. The new order is characterized by the safety of blandness, and the sufficiency of guilt by suspicion.

It is difficult to write against the safety of blandness without a great deal of throat clearing of the 'don't-get-me-wrong' kind. It seems almost *de rigueur to* reiterate every few paragraphs that the point of the work is not to advocate laissez-faire-ism or a return to an old regime. Rather than getting caught in parentheses of this sort, Johnson rightly devotes himself to showing how much is to be gained by understanding "no touch" as a "truth effect" rather than a Truth. No touch is analyzed as a discursive effect of the concept of "child abuse," which is itself discursively organized within a larger regime of truth called "child care." Johnson's work draws attention to a fact we have been allowed to ignore or forget—that is, that child abuse, like self-esteem, is a concept that has been *invented, not discovered.* It is when we forget that self-esteem or child abuse are inventions and treat them as if they were discoveries that we create the conditions in which these terms are most effective in heightening surveillance of the lives of children and their caregivers.

In saying that child abuse has been invented, writers like Johnson are not arguing that children do not suffer physical and mental harm from adults and from each other. Rather, such writers are pointing to the fact that the concept itself is historically constituted, and therefore a more fragile idea than many of us might want to acknowledge. Like self-esteem, child abuse originated in postwar psychotherapy and experimental psychology; both terms have moved since then from being peripheral, theoretical concepts to becoming indispensable to the daily work of teachers, counselors, youth workers, and psychologists. The genealogical approach that Johnson takes, like that of Chris Jenks in *The Postmodern Child* (1996), allows us to understand how child abuse has proliferated its effects as a piece of discourse. This is not the same as saying that incidents of child abuse are "overstated." Rather, it approaches the child-abuse narrative as producing intended and unintended material and social effects in a culture where the reach of its power to categorize is all-pervasive.

Johnson is by no means the only author to raise questions about the pernicious effects of the child-abuse narrative, or to insist on the importance of acknowledging the sexuality of the child. Writing in Australia's national newspaper, journalist Phillip Adams slams the double standards of a culture he sees as engaged in witchhunts about sex and children:

. . . [I]t's okay to have 14-year-olds Pretty Baby'd into fashion models for cover and catwalk. And it's fine for the corporate paedophiles, the giant corporations who molest the childhoods of millions, turning kids into the greediest of consumers. But God forbid that we allow people to . . . look candidly at the issue of child sexuality. In a world where taboos have vanished, it's great to have one that can be dusted off for use by the pious and the hypocritical to advance their political, media or police careers. (1999, 32)

British writer, Stephen Fry, is more subdued but perhaps more troubling in his subversion of the child-abuse narrative. In the autobiography, *Moab is My Washpot* (1997), Fry reflects on his days as a much-punished boy at Uppingham School:

[T]he subject of corporal punishment is so culturally loaded today as to be almost impossible to inspect. It comes in so many people's minds very close to the idea of 'abuse', a word which when used within ten spaces of the word 'child', causes hysteria, madness and stupidity in almost everybody.

. . . If it should so happen that you could prove to me that one of the masters who beat me may have derived sexual gratification from the practice, I would shrug and say, 'Poor old soul, at least he never harmed me'. Abuse is exploitation of trust and exploitation of authority and I was lucky enough never to suffer from that or from any other violation or cruelty, real or imagined. (pp. 86–89)

Fry's reflection indicates that he understands himself to have been beaten but not abused. This is an understanding that is unthinkable to professional child-care workers in the 1990s. So too is the idea that any sexual gratification his teachers might have derived from beating him was not exploitative and deviant. The child-abuse narrative has made this logic, in Fry's own words, "impossible to inspect." It is this truth effect that makes the work of writers like Johnson all the more rare and important.

Over a decade ago, Madeleine Grumet argued that those of us who work with children should not be complicit with "theorists and teachers who repudiate the intimacy of nurture in their own histories and work in education" (1988, p. xvi). Johnson has taken up Grumet's challenge in its fullest sense, by refusing to romanticize or to demonize the child, the caregiver, or the intimate social relations of the act of caring. His documentation compels the reader to confront inherent contradictions in contemporary child-rearing practices. By treating "no

touch" as a discursively organized and historically constituted imperative, he is able to pay attention to discontinuity and ambiguity, and
thereby address more fully "the bitter wisdom of this sweet work"
(Grumet 1988, p. xx) of caregiving.

Erica McWilliam
Associate Professor
Queensland University of Technology

References

Adams, Phillip. 1999. In pursuit of power abusers. *The Weekend Australian Review*, 13–14, February. p. 32.

Baudrillard, Jean. 1979. *Seduction*. Hampshire: Macmillan.

Fry, Stephen. 1997. *Moab is my Washpot*. London: Random House.

Grumet, Madeleine. 1988. *Bitter milk: Women and teaching*. University of Massachusetts: Amherst.

Jenks, Chris. 1996. The Postmodern Child. In *Children and families: Research and policy*, edited by J. Brannen and M. O'Brien. London: Falmer Press.

Tobin, Joe, ed. 1997. *Making a place for pleasure in early childhood*. New Haven and London: Yale University Press.

Acknowledgments

The origins of this book are closely related to several different research projects that I began some five years ago. Initially, my first contact with "no touch" began with the 1994 National Public Radio broadcast "Day Care Center Goes to Extremes to Protect Reputation." At first I didn't want to believe that story and had to go to "extremes" to fully understand the nature of "no touch." Several close colleagues helped me immensely with my initial deliberations of the many critical issues and encouraged me to move forward with my research, including Joe Tobin, Gail Boldt, Donna Grace, and Anne Phelan, all members of a reading group at the University of Hawaii. Several graduate students also assisted me in sorting out my initial perceptions of "no touch," people like Lani Au, Chengua Yang, Felicity McArdle, and Louise Navin pushed me to further critique the many issues which arise out of better understanding this phenomena. As well, to the many hundreds of preservice early childhood and elementary education students in the United States and Australia who listened to my stories and offered their own "no touch" stories, this work would not have been possible to neither begin nor complete without your presence in each of the stories presented here and elsewhere. A special thanks to Erica McWilliam at Queensland University of Technology and Chris Meyers at Peter Lang Publishing who believed in the potential of this story and were instrumental in seeing it come alive on the following pages.

My appreciation to the University of Hawaii for granting a sabbatical leave. My sabbatical stay at Queensland University of Technology in Brisbane, Australia, was extremely vital in helping this book come to fruition. My profound gratitude to Gerald Ashby, Head of School of Early Childhood, for providing the necessary financial support, office space, adjunct faculty status, and opportunities to collaborate with many different faculty, all of which was instrumental in seeing this project off the ground. To my colleagues at QUT, friends like Sue Greishaber, Erica McWilliam, Gordon Tait, Belinda Carpenter and Anna Bower, thank you again for your endless support and incredible hospitality. My visiting seminars at Macquarie University, Griffith University, and the University of Queensland opened my eyes to the many other concerns and issues that colleagues in early childhood education share.

I would like to thank the staff at Peter Lang Publishing, in particular Seth Ditchik and Lisa Dillon for their help in the editing, producing, and promoting of this book.

Some of this work appeared in earlier versions in the chapter "The 'no touch' policy" in Joe Tobin's (ed.), *Making a Place for Pleasure in Early Childhood*. My gratitude to Yale University Press for allowing me permission to include that work here. As well, I owe National Public Radio (broadcast, "Day Care Center Goes to Extremes to Protect Reputation") and King Features (Family Circus comic) gratitude for permission to include their work in this book.

Introduction

Last year in Queensland, Australia, Brisbane's *Courier-Mail* newspaper presented a story entitled, "Sex-Charge Fears Put Men on the Outer" (O'Chee 1997). In this particular story a Year 2 male teacher is said to "live in fear of being labeled a paedophile—just because he's a man" teaching in the primary grades. He revealed that, "if his students try to hug him, he instinctively raises his arms and folds them in defense. If his students come too close while they read, he must try to avoid contact. He can never be alone with a child and if he wants to talk to a student in private, he also asks another three children to stay back" (p. 3).

A few months later, the national paper, *The Australian*, ran an article entitled, "Education Chief Backs Classroom Abuse Watchdog" (Brook and Glascott 1997). In the article the New South Wales Department of Education's Director General said, "We have to probably resign ourselves to the fact that the proportion of paedophiles amongst teachers will be more or less the same as amongst the community as a whole, regrettably." One week later the paper included another related feature story entitled, "Suspicious Minders" (O'Neill 1997). In one part of that story a man discussed walking his dog past a kindergarten and listening to excited children approaching him to inquire about his active pet. He then reported, "Ten years ago I would have stopped and talked to them, let them pat him. That day I gave them a wry grin and walked straight past . . . when he later talked to his male friends about what he had done he decided that his reactions were by no means unique" (p. 9).

An undergraduate student completes a preservice teacher education program noting that he will closely following these "tips" during future classroom interactions with students. He will:

1. Never be alone with a student, male or female, without another teacher or other students around.
2. Never initiate touching a student in any manner unless they indicate in an overt manner that they don't mind it. For example, a student who initiates touching you on the shoulder or arm, or offers a hug, is indicating that he/she does not mind those displays of affection or attention. Of course, certain touching is never appropriate . . . you should never touch "areas where a bathing suit covers you."
3. Never cover up the window on the classroom door. It prohibits administrators and other teachers from looking in, and unless you have something to hide, it's not necessary.
4. Keep the classroom door open as much as possible.
5. Send the child to the nurse if he/she has a problem (such as soiling his or her pants, etc.). If there are other problems in clothing sensitive areas (e.g., belt buckle and pants zipper), elicit the help of a fellow teacher, preferably one of the opposite sex, regardless of the presence of other children.
6. Always hug from the side (avoid frontal hugs whenever possible).
7. Legally, keep a critical incident file for every student.

In 1997, in our weekly Student Teaching Seminar, one of my students, Kahea, discussed a recent incident she experienced in her practica school. Kahea said that as she walked across the playground during recess a fourth grade girl she taught in the previous semester ran up to her and gave her a big hug. Kahea reciprocated this show of affection. Shortly after the child left Kahea was taken aside by the vice principal (VP) and told, "*You should never hug children at this school.*" The VP then took the child aside and instructed her to never *touch* adults like she just had.

Last year in the United States, a national headline story broke about a six-year-old boy, Jonathan Prevette, who kissed a female classmate and was then suspended for "unwarranted and unwelcome touching" (i.e., sexual harassment). Several years ago in the United States, National Public Radio (NPR) included a special within their daily *Morning Edition* newscast titled, "Day Care Center Goes to Extremes to Protect Reputation" (see the appendix for complete transcript). This story mentioned how a day-care center was implementing staff policies that constrained staff from touching children. It described a day-care center in the United States that implemented a "no touch" policy that basically says:

It's against our policy to pick up the kids. It's against our policy to hold them on your lap. The 'no-touch' policy is more to protect the center than the children. In the business of day care, she explains, reputation is everything, and reputation is fragile. It would be too easy, she says, for one innocent hug or playful piggyback ride to be misinterpreted. The picking-up thing, I don't allow, because that's one of those issues where you have, you know, the direct physical contact, body to body, that could be misconstrued, so I—I stop it there. (*Morning Edition*, 1994)

The various stories above reveal an early education profession afflicted with moral panic. As a preschool teacher in the early 1980s I came to know and define myself based on moral panic. I was just settling into a comfortable style of day-to-day caregiver-child interactions, when the massmedia presented television specials and magazine articles (e.g., *Newsweek's* May 1984 cover story) on child sexual abuse. This sudden creation of a social problem by the mass media operated to "reinforce and give shape to the crowd's (societal) sense of expectancy and provide the content of rumours and shared definitions with which ambiguous situations were restructured" (Cohen 1973, p. 451).

What a stifling effect this moral panic held over a young male teacher who until this time worried mostly about establishing warm, trusting relationships with all the children in his care. Suddenly many of my once typical daily teacher-child interactions took on a new dimension. I began to perceive myself in a much different way, a way defined and guided by someone/something else much more powerful than any one individual. As a teacher I started to worry and second-guess myself when I went about my once taken-for-granted routines of changing diapers, wiping runny noses, unbuttoning and buttoning a two-year-old's "Button Down 501" jeans, and supervising a group of several three-year-old girls involved in outdoor sprinkler play as they frolicked about clothed only in their underpants. I wondered about holding and attempting to calm an out-of-control three-year-old in a "football hold," as I was skillfully instructed to do during my master's practica.

Suddenly, the sense of touch, which has always been such an integral part of my relationship with children (my own or any other I care for) was being called into question. What I did with those questions is what haunts me now and what led me to focus my work on this project. At the time, I accepted the fact that a larger force (again, this overwhelming sense of moral panic) was changing the way I interacted with children. I mostly gave in and did little to fight it. The recent "no touch" developments in early education have awakened personal memories of my early years as a teacher. This time I feel compelled to act, before the "no touch" policy, which is becoming more prevalent and familiar in school contexts each day, overwhelms us, intimidating yet another generation of teachers.

At a time in our society when issues of physical touch come to the forefront of how we can and can't interact with young children (Bantick 1997), this work interrogates "no touch" policies in education today. This book is grounded initially with the introduction of a variety of "no touch" stories from the field of early childhood/primary education. These stories are then critiqued through the lenses of moral panic, as each case represents an obvious systematic mechanism of social control, created and supported by all of us.

These stories, gathered from a variety of settings (i.e., university classrooms, electronic user groups, lecture halls, conference settings, school visits, preschool and primary classroom sites, and books, journals, and newspapers) represent a collection of different sources, but share a common thread. They represent the multitude of collective voices of those who care for young children, caregiver's and teacher's, early childhood and elementary preservice and graduate student's, school principal's and child-care director's, voices from professional literature and research, and parents'. Because much of the research was conducted during my sabbatical stay at Queensland University of Technology, in Brisbane, Australia, both Australian and American voices are represented in this work.

In the first chapter I situate the reader in "no touch" as a construct and discuss the role of the caregiver/teacher in the care of young children, especially related to their traditionally constructed role as "nurturant" providers. My personal subjectivity as a nurturant caregiver is critiqued in the last part of this chapter. Chapter 2 builds on the now-common stories of "no touch," using moral panic as a construct to interrogate further the implications of program policies that disallow teachers from physically interacting with children in early and primary education. Critiquing these current stories of social control and surveillance by using the historical works of Stanley Cohen, Stuart Hall, and other current sociological theorists, reveal just how firmly the moral panic is rooted in our psyche.

Drawing heavily on the earlier discussion of social control, chapter 3 uses teacher case studies to reveal how prevalent the moral panic of "no touch" is, as it has entered both professional and personal contexts. I chose to use a wide variety of stories here to capture "the richness of indeterminacy of our experiences as teachers and the complexity of our understandings of what teaching is and how others can be prepared to engage in this profession" (Carter 1993). After presenting and critiquing these teacher/caregiver stories this chapter then presents and critiques other related "no touch" narratives, such as: classrooms with video cameras in each room; child-care center policies on diapering that disallow men from diapering children; and inservice sessions that show staff how to appropriately hold children on their lap.

Chapter 4 works in opposition to the discussion of social control, instead illustrating how some teachers are actively teaching against the moral panic of "no touch" and attempting to counter its potential negative effect in their classrooms. Drawing on case study examples from teachers, the stories this chapter interrogates include examples of "touch" from teachers and researchers at the Touch Research Institute, who strongly advocate for the inclusion of touch in their daily caregiving practices.

It has become impossible to think of such issues as identity, power, and politics without an understanding of sexuality. Revisiting the sexuality issues evident throughout most of the earlier chapters and moving away from moral panic, chapter 5 reconceptualizes "no touch" by theoretically juxtaposing it around issues of identity and representation, issues of sexuality.

Recognizing that the personal voices of children are left out of this particular project, chapter 6 calls on the reader to utilize self-inquiry processes to assist in "visualizing" the many issues of "no touch" that directly impact children. Suggesting that this personal reflection might be quite helpful in moving out of "no touch," the chapter later suggests that addressing emotionally responsive care can help us better understand the full extent of what it means to not touch, not nurture, those children we care for.

In the closing chapter I consider where we are today with "no touch" and question how this policy has influenced our lives as caregivers, social workers, parents, teachers, and policymakers. I ask that we think past moral panic as a construct that assisted in the earlier interrogation of "no touch." Because moral panics are said to disappear just as quickly as they appear, their representational presence can be obscured as a site of permanent struggle. Given this, "no touch" itself runs the risk of being enveloped within the disappearing moral panic, to be forgotten as quickly as it was instated.

Chapter 1

Touch or "No Touch"

Touch is the relating force, unique in the universe. Touch lies situated behind breath, blood, and the vibration of the nervous system. Touch brings each function into contact with the presence lying beyond but passing through the vessel of the body. The body is brought to touch because touch predates the body.
—David Appelbaum, *The Interpenetrating Reality*

Truth is a thing of this world: it is produced only by virtue of multiple forms of constraint. And it induces regular effects of power. Each society has its regime of truth, its "general politics" of truth: that is, the types of discourse which it accepts and makes function as true; the mechanism and instances which enable one to distinguish true and false statements, the means by which each is sanctioned; the techniques and procedures accorded value in the acquisition of truth; the status of those who are charged with saying what counts as true.
—Michel Foucault, "What is enlightenment?"

Like most caregivers and preschool teachers my teaching practices have been heavily influenced by my experiential work with young children and by what I formally studied and learned in a teacher education program. In fact, during my undergraduate and graduate studies, most of what I learned about the care of children was centered around the importance of touch, as a way of building a warm and trusting relationship with each child in my care. To assist in my initial learning of the importance of being a nurturant, warm, and supportive caregiver (Spodek and Saracho 1994), my professors guided me through the historical work on Harlow's attachment studies, Spitz's work on hospitalism and adult-infant interactions, Bowlby's work on maternal deprivation, and Klaus and Kennell's research on parent-infant bonding. These various works related the importance of touch to healthy physiological and psychological growth (Brazelton 1984). All the research I read and discussed in class stressed the critical relationship of early stimulation (especially skin-to-skin touch) and the child's later healthy development (Klaus and Kennell 1976). As well, I learned about the damage that can be caused from inadequately formed adult-child relationships (Montagu 1978).

Building on much of these earlier studies, the latest infant research reveals that skin-to-skin contact helps infants in general and premature infants in particular sleep longer, gain more weight, breathe more regularly, nurse more successfully, and achieve a stable heart rate (Field 1990; Jones 1994; LaForge 1994). Scafidi et alia's research on preterm infants (1996) suggests that they gain 47 percent more weight, become more responsive, are discharged six days earlier at a hospital cost savings of $10,000 per infant (or $4.7 billion if the 470,000 preemies born each year are massaged). Some of the most recent research on preschool age children reveals that children who receive massages fall asleep sooner, exhibit more restful naptime periods and have decreased activity levels. Massage therapy decreased the anxiety, depression, and cortisol levels (a stress hormone) of children who survived Hurricane Andrew. In addition, their drawings became less depressed. Following five thirty-minute massages these children/adolescents had better sleep patterns, lower depression, anxiety and stress hormone levels (cortisol and norepinephrine), and better clinical progress (Touch Research Institute 1997).

At that time in my career my pedagogical practices were steeped in the cultivation of the sensory-rich classroom, as I attempted to enact "hands-on" learning by allowing children to work with an assortment of manipulatives, build with blocks, touch sand and water at the water table, and experience a wide variety of sensorial materials in the Play Doh and clay table. Incorporating what I had learned about touch and the caring encounter into my daily classroom practices seemed quite natural, and I felt like a good caregiver because of my "touching" pedagogical practices. In retrospect, I felt very much like the type of caregiver Dittman (1986) describes: "A good caregiver is loving and responsive. One who hugs, rocks, cuddles, seeks eye contact, and enjoys the child . . . who responds to the baby's smiles and emerging skills and interests . . . who finds ways to expand upon each experience . . . is sociable and interested" (p. 43). I left school firmly believing that "Hugs, loving touches, and lap-sitting are generally recognized components of high quality early childhood programs" (Hyson, Whitehead, and Prudhoe 1988, p. 55)

When I think back now to what my daily physical interactions/ touches were like (what Alice Honig calls the "sensuous nature of inti- mate ministrations," 1989), I recall guiding two-year-olds to help clean up with a supportive touch on the back as they sought to run else- where; I remember tickling infants during play or diaper changing; giving children warm pats on the back; readily accepting children onto my lap during story time; physically removing and then holding ag- gressive first-graders so they couldn't harm themselves or others; and tousling children's hair while joking with them. I recall that many of the physical teaching experiences I shared with children are those same nurturant practices I now incorporate into my daily parental interactions with my own children. Some of the fondest memories I have of those early teaching experiences are intimate memories that surround the physical touch(ing) of the children I cared for.

As an early childhood education teacher educator I am very much interested in how teachers today physically interact with children in their care. In my research work during the past few years I've inter- viewed numerous groups of preservice early childhood teachers, fo- cusing specifically on the question, "As a teacher, in what ways will you be touching your students?" I was mostly pleased to find that the expectations my students today have for physically interacting with children mirror my preschool teaching experiences many years ago. When asked how they think they will be touching children in their care, my students shared the following examples:

> . . . cuddle to comfort; pat on back affirmation; touch them to show support; hold hands; arm around shoulder; through hugs; gentle pats; changing dia- pers; hold hands on excursions; reassuring children through holding them; to assist through traumatic separation from parent(s) some children will need holding; cuddle if they are upset; administering first aid if a child hurts self; tucking clothes in and investigating an injury; arrival and departure hugs and high 5's; dressing, feeding and toileting; restraining children for their own safety; to direct them to go somewhere touch on shoulder; during gross motor activities I will hold hands to help balance, jump, slide pole, etc.; hold babies if distressed; push on swing or help up into a swing; spontaneous cuddles; hygiene; rubbing and patting back and stroking hair to help child get to sleep; having children on my lap during carpet time; patting their head in recogni- tion or praise; behavior management; playing outdoors; remove a child who poses a danger to others; and during game playing, like tag.

Again, the expectations these teachers share are closely aligned with my notions of how we're *supposed to* physically interact with young children in our care, my notions of touch in early education

(Johnson 1997a). These notions are closely aligned with popular notions of supportive child development pedagogical practices. For example, Mazur and Pekor (1985) note that, "Cuddles and hugs, physical care-taking . . . are all part of the daily experience shared between infants and toddlers and their caregivers. This nurturance helps to create and sustain the trusting relationships which enable children to feel secure and to become autonomous" (p. 11).

As I mentioned, I don't remember a day of work with two-year-olds when I did not exchange some kind of meaningful touch with a child in my care. I always remember the joy of touch when as a preschool teacher I changed diapers, rocked children to sleep, and let them sit on my lap during story time. Even during my encounters with older, school-age children (while directing an inner-city school-age child-care center), touch was also an integral part of all our collective staff-child relationships. For me, as for many who care for young children, touch is viewed as an "authentic" (Slunt 1994), natural way of *being* with children in my care (one of the many ways I feel *connected* with children). Appelbaum (1988) explains this notion of the interpenetrability of touch as such:

> In the free interchange between the world and ourself through the body membrane, touch is the herald of existence. Until touch is inclusive enough to embrace the contrary, we are not sufficiently acted upon by a penetrating reality . . . the interpenetrability of touch binds the cosmos, ourselves and the world, in its togetherness . . . [this] love of contact engenders contact. (pp. 160–175)

Duty of Care

As is expected of all teachers and caregivers, when I assumed the role of teacher in each of the early childhood education settings where I worked, I assumed a professional role, and along with that professional responsibilities. An integral part of those professional responsibilities included the provision of nurturance for all the children in my care. As an example, as part of the minimum professional standards a person must meet to be a licensed teacher in the State of Hawaii, the Hawaii Teacher Standards Board (1998) requires (among other things) all teachers to: Nurture students' desire to learn and achieve; Promote empathy, compassion and mutual respect among students; and Model a caring attitude and promote positive interpersonal relationships.

Building on the theoretical work I was examining in the university, as a professional early childhood teacher—a caretaker of young children—I came to believe that touch was part of my physical "duty of care" and of high value in the formation of healthy human development for the children I cared for, and for my own healthy development. My everyday adult-child interactions helped to shape my understanding of self, and self as teacher, and in fact because of these interactions touch grew to be a vital aspect of my pedagogical practices. This way of being professional in the teacher-student relationship is proximal to Slunt's (1994) notion of the caregiver-patient relationship in the health field, as she says,

> Nurses and educators are privileged to have the ongoing, daily opportunity to affect the lives of others. In working with both patients and students, we are in close physical proximity to making a difference. In coming face to face we take the first step towards creating an enduring interpersonal bond, one that is capable of withstanding physical separation. An enduring bond is sustained through an authentic relationship. (p. 57)

A large part of the "authenticity" of the caregiver-child relationship involves nurturance, or "fostering the development of another" (Melson, Fogel, and Powell 1988, p. 57). In the care of young children, the provision of emotional, social, and physical (through touch) nurturance is the social expectation as the caregiver (professional) operates within a "profession characterized by interaction and responsibility for others" (Slunt 1994, p. 60). I would argue that this is true of all teacher-student relationships, but even more so in the primary and elementary education fields, where teachers enter the profession because they like interacting with this age group and they want to work with (academically) and nurture the children in their care.

My Perceptions of Teacher as Toucher

From all that I had read and studied and from all I learned during my classroom interactions with children, I believed, like Katz (1989) that,

> . . . we must give precedence to touch over all other senses because its perceptions have the most compelling character of reality. Touch plays a far greater role than do the other senses in the development of belief in the reality of the external world. (p. 240)

As a novice teacher the multiple discourses I confronted were comfortable and matched what seemed to me my natural style of interacting with children. Then I soon confronted a society that was burdened with the moral panic of sexual abuse, and I allowed this to negatively influence my sense of self as a teacher. In an apolitical sense, with little intellectual engagement I willingly participated in the larger political process inherent in this moral panic (Casey 1993). Passively, I defined myself and was defined by and within these discourses. I was learning how to position myself correctly within the popular "no touch" movement, created and pronounced by others.

Bronwyn Davies' (1993) work on discourse analysis is effective in revealing the power of discourse in shaping individual subjectivities. While learning the patterns of desire appropriate for them, Davies argues that individuals, "Discover what positions are available to members . . . and how to live the detail of those positionings as they come to understand and take up as their own particular patterns of desire relevant to them" (p. 145).

Critiquing Davies work helped me understand how my positioning as a male teacher of young children shifted during the moral panic (which is addressed fully in the next chapter). In Davies' terms, I "took up the subject positions made available" to me. These discourses instilled by powerful others (mass media; the conservative right; various early education professional associations; popular literature) guaranteed that my "ways of knowing children" were defined and dictated by those others, who are actively involved in the continuing moral panic centered around how teachers of young children touch their students. I witness similar "shifts" occurring now as I watch the current moral panic of child abuse work to change teacher subjectivities today. These more recent accounts of touch in early schooling are informing teachers and children that they should both incorporate and follow written and unwritten "no touch" guidelines during their daily experiences with each other (Johnson 1997b). This is readily evident in the many teacher stories included here.

Shifting Discourses of Touch

Similar to the earlier question I posed to some Australian early childhood students several years ago ("As a teacher, in what ways will you be touching your students?"), I just recently polled another group of American undergraduate early childhood students, asking them to explain why they think children need physical attention and touch for their growth. Among other things, the responses generally reflected that the theoretical perspectives being taught today closely mirror those theories I learned as an undergraduate and graduate student in child development and early childhood education. Reflecting the relative constancy of early childhood theoretical perspectives about the importance of touch, among other things the students said children need touch for their emotional and physical growth. Issues about the importance of attachment and bonding were mentioned in the majority of responses. Many respondents mentioned the importance of "building trust" while learning about relationships through touch. As well, several students shared that children need to feel loved and secure in a caregiver-child relationship and touch provides an important avenue for helping to establish those feelings (e.g., a teacher shared, "As I recall young children must have warm, loving, and nurturing relationships to provide the conditions that free them to grow and learn that the world is a trustworthy place"). Other descriptive words the teachers used which shared some commonality include "nurturing," "safe," "accepted," and "comforting." This group of teachers expressed common beliefs and assumed a common sense of responsibility for conveying an important message to themselves and others, the message that touch is an important part of their work in the care of children.

These students are learning that touch is the first experience in the world for the newborn and that the neonate first comes to know the primary caregiver through tactile response (Jones 1994). Touch provides a one-of-a-kind stimulation that can't be replicated in any manner. As mentioned earlier, from the very beginning moments of life touch provides the necessary security for later healthy psychological development. Like previous research, Heller's work (1997) illustrates that touch:

> . . . stimulates physical and mental growth; assures smoothness of physiological functions like breathing, heart rate, and digestion; enhances their self-concept, body awareness, and sexual identity; boosts their immune system; and even enhances the grace and stability of their movement. (p. 5)

In studying popular research and literature like Heller's, preservice early childhood teachers, be they American, Australian, or Taiwanese, are learning that touch in the care of children is highly significant. Yet even while people like me teach the importance of touch in the academy, and even while our early childhood students profess the importance of touch in their practices, when theory meets practice in the classroom much is lost in the exchange. Suddenly, the preservice teacher who stressed that touch for infants is "very necessary," will, in the next breath (just short of a formal recant) express that threats of being accused of child abuse make her so nervous she won't change a diaper. Another student who readily shares her belief in the role of touch in establishing a safe and secure mother-child attachment, will just as readily express that she does not allow children to sit in her lap, for any reason. Another teacher shares that touch is "very important" and yet she works in a school where a male teacher "can't do many things" like changing diapers. Lastly, while expressing her belief that touch helps build a sense of connection between teacher and child, one teacher shared that while on a recent field trip to the beach teachers were instructed not to touch any child's chest or genital areas to assist in the removal of sticky sand. This was fine with the teacher as she did not want to be accused of any inappropriate interactions.

Theorizing "No Touch" Discourse

"No touch" has become too familiar to me, and while I'm somewhat surprised at this familiarity I really shouldn't be. Being surprised allows for the possibility that happenstance had something to do with this familiarity. Foucault said the "production of discourse is at once controlled, selected, organized and redistributed by a certain number of procedures whose role is to ward off its powers and dangers, to gain mastery of its chance events" (1981, p. 52). It is the continuous repetition of like stories, like discourses, that both disturbs me and compels me to further consider the popularity of "no touch" policies and practices today. I'm interested in the commonality of these practices as they mirror the extent to which forces in our culture have debilitated (Heller 1997) once-common parent-child, teacher-child, and child-child physical, social, and emotional interactions.

To reveal the "commonality" of "no touch" and the "forces in our culture that have debilitated," this book presents a multiplicity of narratives that simultaneously relate to touch and "no touch." At times these stories are critically interrogated through different critical analyses, at other times they are left to the reader to personalize and critique in a way they see fit. When different critical perspectives are used in the analyses they tend to be framed around a poststructural perspective, a perspective which insists that "no touch" discourse is simultaneously contingent, multiply determined, and constantly shifting (Todd 1997). In this regard, as a collective, the "no touch" narratives shared here and in other texts reveal, "There is no single ['no touch'] 'truth', only different constructions, different representations, some of which are read as 'fact', some as 'fiction', depending on the way they are functionally contextualized and by whom and in whose interests" (Threadgold 1990, p. 3).

I purposely chose a broad collection of "no touch" stories, most of which are verbatim written accounts gleaned from multiple sources, others which are oral accounts, transcribed and re-written with the editorial license granted to any author. Using a poststructuralist approach to writing, the stories or data that I present are not necessarily meant to support an analysis (although the overly trained conservative structuralist side of me feels they do in many cases), but instead, "demonstratively and perfomatively" (Lather 1991, p. 106) deconstruct "no touch." Rhedding-Jones (1996) defines deconstructions as "poststructural ways of examining discourses and texts as operating in relation to each other" (p. 28), and then illustrates that deconstructing "involves a series of readings against the usual meanings of data" (p. 29). There is no single "no touch" story that captures the essence of this phenomena or that proves or disproves its existence.

The poststructuralist style of research and writing here allows the reader to work through all of the presented texts and subtexts, which are intentionally juxtaposed "by a range of genres, by addressing decentred reading audiences within the text, by layering meanings, and by the occasional personal inclusion in the research of the writer's voice and body" (Rhedding-Jones, 1996, p. 29). Like a novelist, these stories are presented here as a "collage of recordings made at the moments of happening and at the later times of reflection . . . the artistry of language lies in the selections and presentations, and not in a scientific representation or finding" (p. 30).

Always the stories shared here are witnessed as embedded in a "complex machinery for producing discourses" (Carrington and Bennett 1996). Even though the stories may stand alone on a page, indented within a paragraph, embedded within a minor or major section of the text, along Foucaultian (1980) lines, the many stories expressed here are positioned within a much larger "grid of judgements, measurements and critiques"—for alongside every "no touch" story exist a multiplicity of (an)other "touch" stories. To reveal how discourses like "no touch" are intricately produced and to interrogate their evolution Tobin (1997) illustrates that by using Foucault's grid of power and knowledge we

> Chart contemporary beliefs and practices . . . [and] we must examine a range
> of texts, including television specials and newspaper headlines, proceedings
> of courts and Congress, academic journals and child-rearing manuals, poli-
> cies of child protective services and the insurance industry. (p. 3)

Any genealogical descriptions of policies like "no touch" must be broad enough to trace (Jóhannesson 1998) how far reaching the related issues extend, as these processes inherently inquire, "how did series of discourses come to be formed, across the grain of, in spite of, or with the aid of these systems of constraints; what was the specific norm of each one, and what were their conditions of appearance, growth, variation" (Foucault 1981, p. 70). The historical production and continued reproduction of "no touch" involves, among diverse other issues, different ways of thinking, different understandings and interpretations of children, adults, and the moral, social, and political spheres they occupy. To indicate the depth of the debate and the extent of "oppositional discourses" (Becket 1996) this book proceeds in the analytical style Tobin suggests above, as I compiled, presented, and then interrogated a wide range of texts, including radio and television specials, newspaper headlines, court cases, popular early childhood education textbooks and journals, electronic list serve postings, and first-hand stories from teachers, parents, and administrators. Like other genealogical research, through the course of this compilation, presentation and interrogation of "no touch" my work here "studies conjunctures of discourses, searches for ruptures and breaks in social practices, and identifies the formation of new historical conjunctures" (Jóhannesson 1998, p. 304).

Just as I did in my research, by introducing and interrogating a range of texts the reader is assisted in the process of looking deeper into the "no touch" discourse, or "the practice in which people reproduce relations of power (both subjugation and domination), at the same time as they sustain shared culture" (Lindstrom 1990, p. 20). Continuing on to chapter 2 and hopefully throughout the rest of this text, as a reader you now offer your own poststructuralist perspective(s). Your further close reading/interrogation of my writing, by definition, insists on new understandings of "no touch" as each new interpretive understanding creates new narratives.

Chapter 2

"No Touch" as Moral Panic

*. . . these categories work to protect the individual from a partially per-
ceived threat of diversity and conflict . . . Hence the repetition of moral
panics, their fundamentally serial nature, the infinite variety of tone and
posture which they can assume. The successful policing of desire requires
that we think of "the enemy" everywhere, and at all times.*
—Simon Watney, *Policing Desire*

*Intimate touch beckons. Yet we refuse response to the need to be. We
betray the call to embody consciousness at the bridging point between
levels of reality. Is there a substance to our refusal?*
—David Appelbaum, *The Interpenetrating Reality*

The purpose of this chapter is to illustrate just how powerful and far-
reaching the moral panic of "no touch" is in early and primary education today. Beginning with Stuart Hall's work I will illustrate how moral
panics work to create and support mechanisms of social control. Stuart
Hall and his colleagues' (1978) interpretation of this phenomenon
helps me identify and understand my place in the "no touch" moral
panic, as they state:

> When the official reaction to a person, groups of persons or series of events
> is out of all proportion to the actual threat offered, when 'experts', in the
> form of police chiefs, the judiciary, politicians and editors perceive the threat
> in all but identical terms, and appear to talk 'with one voice' of rates, diag-
> noses, prognoses and solutions, when the media representations universally
> stress 'sudden and dramatic' increases (in numbers involved or events) and
> 'novelty', above and beyond that which a sober, realistic appraisal could sus-
> tain, then we believe it is appropriate to speak of the beginnings of a moral
> panic. (p. 16)

As described here, the recent James Bulger case in England is a classic example of what Hall et alia's research depicted:

James Bulger was a month short of his third birthday when two killers lured him away from his mother in a busy shopping mall, dragged him to a lonely railway embankment and murdered him. It was an unspeakably cruel death. The thought of anyone being cruel enough to inflict such a fate on an innocent little child defies comprehension. Astonishingly, the killers in this case were both just ten years old. (Jenks 1996, p. 118)

A similar example is the 1998 death of a child in Scandinavia, a tragedy which reportedly occurred as a result of an older child subjecting a younger child to numerous violent and aggressive karate kicks (supposedly modeled on one of the popular television Power Rangers), leading to the immediate ban of *Power Rangers* on national television.

More recently, the Chicago case where two boys (ages ten and eleven) bullied and then killed a five-year-old boy (by dropping him out of a fourteenth-floor apartment) was lobbied to the public as an "advance warning system" seemingly about children in general. The State's Attorney initiated the panic by saying, "It's *Lord of the Flies* on a massive scale . . . We've become a nation being terrorized by our children" (Annin 1996, p. 57). The mass media (*Newsweek* magazine in this case) then further spread the panic by presenting this case to the world with a January 22, 1996, story heading that read, "Superpredators Arrive: Should We Cage the New Breed of Vicious Kids?" And so a onetime "scene" is presented as an all-consuming "movement" as the media tries to create a self-fulfilling prophecy out of a cover story (McRobbie and Thornton 1995). As Fass (1997) notes, stories like these illustrate how the media is able to "create an audience hungry for more" (Heller 1998).

Much less tragic, but nonetheless related, examples include the recent cases in different United Kingdom schools, one in which staff contest that an unruly ten-year-old is making it impossible to teach the rest, while staff at another school insist that sixty pupils are unteachable. "It is as though the devil's own spawn have overrun Britain's classrooms, and are ripping apart the very fabric of society . . . and once a moral panic gets started, evidence gets flattened by an avalanche of anecdotes" (*Economist* 1996, p. 57). Stories such as these are matched by the now all-too-common stories from teachers in the United States, teachers who state that they can't possibly teach the MTV/video generation child(ren) without introducing similar high-stimulus, performative pedagogical procedures as those witnessed on television and video.

Stories like these, which depict children as incapable of logical thought and potentially evil, abound in historical and current literature (Cheeseman 1994; deMause 1974; Schorsch 1979; Stoler 1996). Each of the previous cases, and the thousands of other told and untold cases like them, depict children and childhood in oppositional discourses to those with which we are most familiar. The way that childhood has been traditionally constructed and "packaged" (Cheeseman 1994; Steinberg and Kincheloe 1997) in this century has led us to visualize the child[ren] as:

> . . . a form of 'nostalgia', a longing for times past, not as 'futurity'. Children are now seen not so much as 'promise' but as primary and unequivocal sources of love, but also as partners in the most fundamental, unchosen, unnegotiated form of relationship. (Jenks 1996, pp. 106–107)

When popular notions like these are shattered by alternate stories of children and childhood under assault (Stephens 1993), we immediately seek to retrieve their/our innocence by addressing the prevailing moral panic. Journalistic practices now incorporate moral panics as a common way of attracting the attention to the public, as a way of "orchestrating consent by actively intervening in the space of public opinion and social consciousness through the use of highly emotive and rhetorical language which has the effect of requiring that 'something be done about it'" (McRobbie and Thornton 1995, p. 562).

Stanley Cohen's (1972) description of moral panic is assistive in grounding the development of "no touch" in early childhood education. He writes:

> . . . a condition, episode, person or groups of persons emerges to become defined as a threat to societal values and interests; its nature is presented in a stylized and stereotypical fashion by the mass media; the moral barricades are manned by editors, bishops, politicians and other right-thinking people . . . Sometimes the panic passes over and is forgotten, except in folk-lore and collective memory; at other times it has more serious and long-lasting repercussions and might produce such changes as those in legal and social policy or even in the way that society perceives itself. (p. 9)

A variety of moral panics have presented themselves in recent history. In the past several years the panic over AIDS, disallowing lesbian women from receiving intrauterine sperm fertilization, legalizing same sex marriages, the removal of federal dollars to school districts that use curriculum materials that teach about homosexuality, and the blanket statement that violence on television makes children violent, could all be viewed as moral panics (Johnson 1997e). McRobbie and Thornton (1995) also view the "immorality of young people, the absence of parental control, the problem of too much free time leading to crime, and the threat which deviant behavior poses to national identity" (p. 561) as moral panics that reappear with "startling regularity." Jenkins (1992) feels that moral panic has been usefully applied to describe British "dole scroungers" or welfare cheats, and pornography campaigns and censorship.

In the following narrative case we can see the enactment of a moral panic for caregivers of young children. A popular child-care journal article entitled, "The New Untouchables: Risk Management of Child Abuse in Child Care," suggest steps for the child-care administrator to follow to protect the center against unforeseen accusations of child abuse. Among their suggestions are, "Where possible, try to have at least two adults with the children at all times. If this is not always possible, try to keep the single caregiver time to a minimum and where possible, rotate those who are left alone with the children" (Strickland and Reynolds 1988, p. 20).

Such suggestions as these take on different coloration as they become an enacted discourse for all readers. Law-burdened discourse tends to become center policy with little consideration for how that policy affects the wider early childhood field, in a potentially dangerous manner (Murray and McClure 1996). In their concern for prevention, the authors, like much of society, are too quick to rush to judgment (Platt 1995). We're readily reminded of this in a recent *Newsweek* cover story that discusses the "fevered pitch" with which America today addresses claims of child abuse. As Nowesnick (1993) points out, "We haven't done very well at preventing it, but we're frantic to root it out and stomp it to death no matter where it lurks—or doesn't."

The McMartin Preschool case is a perfect example of this. In the summer of 1983, a mother of a preschool boy at the McMartin Preschool in California, informed the local police that her son was being sexually abused while in the care of several teachers at the preschool. Among other vivid accounts she told the police that:

> The teacher, Ray Buckey, had held her son's head in a toilet while he sodomized him. Wearing a mask and cape, he taped the boy's eyes, mouth and hands, and stuck an air tube up his rectum. He had made the boy ride naked on a horse, and he himself had dressed up as a child-molesting cop, a fireman, a clown, and a Santa Claus. She said that teachers at the school had jabbed

scissors into the boy's eyes, and put staples in his ears, nipples, and tongue; Ray had pricked the boy's finger and put it in a goat's anus; she also claimed that three women at the preschool were witches who had buried her son in a coffin; and one of them had killed a real baby, chopped open the head, and burned the brains. (Money 1995, p. 86)

The boy whom Buckey reportedly abused had attended the school for a total of only fourteen days, and had been supervised by Ray Buckey only twice. The woman who made these claims, a known alcoholic suffering from acute schizophrenia, died three years later from an alcohol-related illness. Seven years from the initial claim, three years after the trial officially commenced (the longest criminal case in the history of the United States), $20 million and 55,000 court document pages later, the state prosecution lost this case as the jury acquitted all staff who had been indicted. And yet the irreparable damage was already done, as the McMartin Preschool staff, children, parents, and, ultimately, all those other people who care for children in out-of-home settings like the McMartin Preschool, would now be seen and treated as somehow different.

I know this experience of feeling "different" as a caregiver. This was at a time when issues like serial murder, child sex rings, child abduction, and ritualized child abuse was of heightened concern to the American public (Jenkins 1992). In the early 1980s, as a new teacher working with two and three-year-old children, I first experienced moral panic when reported child sexual abuse cases in school settings (e.g., the McMartin Preschool) made national headlines. Suddenly my physical interactions with children during toileting times, during nap time, or out on the playground were suspect, with my own watchful gaze the primary vehicle of self-inspection. Without anyone directly telling me, I allowed the contagion of moral panic to affect how I touched, or failed to touch children (Mikkelsen 1997). In the same way that Hall et alia (1978) illustrated how more people in England saw themselves as potential mugging victims after muggings were cast as a moral panic by the media, I too felt my own "sense of 'trust' and security had been undermined" (p. 20). From all that I am observing and hearing today, the moral panic in early childhood education appears even stronger now, threatening all that we are about as individuals, as caregivers of young children, and as members of the field of early childhood education.

As much as individuals and groups try to reduce and dismiss the moral panic of "no touch," reports from the field suggest that we have in fact let the moral panic irrationally define us and (mis)guide our understandings of children and how we interact with and relate to them.

Children

Our understandings and interpretations of children and childhood are dominated by rather traditional, nostalgic notions of that period in our own lives, a period, for most of us, now marked by a distance of several decades. Bennett's (1979) review of childhood is helpful here, as he shares:

> Childhood is reminiscence and imagination . . . a child represents complete freedom to think as one pleases, to live in a world where things can and do happen for no reason at all, where good and bad, right and wrong, up and down just don't exist. Who wouldn't prefer such a place. (p. 24)

We treat children as ever-innocent, protection-starved individuals and we treat ourselves as benevolent, overprotective, redemptive humanitarians, always on the ready to provide needed child interventions (Robertson 1997). This romantic premise with which we acknowledge children as marginalized beings and childhood as a marginalized period, assists with our propensity to protect children so willfully, and to accept moral panic(s) so willingly. As vigilant protectors, as saviors, we rush to make preconceived judgments about the sanctity of children and childhood with seemingly little concern for how that interaction impacts children's lives (Holt 1975; Kitzinger 1997; O'Hagan and Dillenburger 1995). Our protective vigilance leads us, as "child savers" to intervene in the lives of children in the following ways: "Sick children require medical care, rebellious children call for legal controls, deprived children need a social welfare system, while innocent child victims require expanded child protective services, and judicial and legislative changes to facilitate children's involvement in the courts" (Stephens 1993, p. 250). And so, when the media interrupts our daily lives with lucid tales of sexual abuse in child care centers or wild children rampaging through classrooms (e.g., *Lord of the Flies* gone awry) we immediately seek to counter these stories (by "control[ing] and rewrite[ing] sexuality in a way that distances [us] adults from children and alienates us . . ." [Silin 1997 p. 223]), these moral panics, with our zeal for savioristic attitudes (Stephens 1993).

With little intellectual rigor we address only the immediate problem, by rapidly creating a moral panic and then quickly eradicating it (always setting ourselves up as the vigilant, concerned adults and keeping the children forever innocent, therefore, always in need of intervention. So on those very very remote occasions when child abuse is witnessed in a day-care center, the rapid spread of the inevitable moral panic warrants that it must be happening in all day-care centers, unless we implement measures to control it, at all costs (e.g., implementing center policies that disallow male caregivers from changing diapers; telling all teachers they must keep classroom doors and window shades open at all times; installing video cameras in classrooms). These control measures act to bring purification back to the caregivers, the scapegoats, so that they are effectively cleaned of "contamination and reinstated as clean in their own eyes . . ." (Douglas 1995, p. 14). More important, we continue promoting the facade that because of our actions all children are now safer (Ramelli 1997).

Measures like this make all of us feel good, all the time, as we then know we've acted responsibly, we've done our duty to intervene in the lives of the innocent children, and we're now protecting them (as always) and their natural state (and ultimately the Nation and the State), whether or not they need our services (Chadwick 1994; Shamgar-Handelman 1994; Hendrick 1997; Qvortrup 1994). The ever-changing nature of adult work and life in our unstable, late-modern society has led us to visualize and use children in curious ways.

Jenks believes that, "We need children as the sustainable, reliable, trustworthy, now outmoded treasury of social sentiments that they have come to represent" (1996, p. 108). Even while adult partners come and go, the child always stays as the last remaining, irrevocable, unexchangeable primary relationship (Beck 1992). This nostalgic view of their essence is part of a complex, late-modern, rearguard attempt at resolving much of what is wrong with our own collective adult lives, as we mourn for our own past childhoods while envious of the children now experiencing it (Cheeseman 1994). And so as our own adult lives tragically fail we shift the focus of attention to the children, becoming "their protectors and nurturers . . . [while] they have become our primary love objects, our human capital and our future" (Jenks 1996, p. 99).

We've gone to great lengths to illustrate that children are innocent, vulnerable, and in constant need of saving, so much so that childhood is our most "intensively governed sector of personal existence" (Rose 1990, p. 121). In his book, *Governing the Soul*, Rose extends this argument by stating,

> . . . the modern child has become the focus of innumerable projects that
> purport to safeguard it from physical, sexual, or moral danger, to ensure its
> 'normal' development, to actively promote certain capacities of attributes such
> as intelligence, educability, and emotional stability . . . anxieties concerning
> children have occasioned a panoply of programmes that have tried to con-
> serve and shape children by moulding the petty details of the domestic, con-
> jugal, and sexual lives of their parents. (p. 121)

We enhance our need to intervene and to protect children by responding to the "real live" reports from the front lines, reports that
typically portray children as continually in need of our services. When
research articles begin with language like, "Young children today face
a world that is more dangerous than at any time in history" (Hollander
1992), we then immediately know our place, and we assume that redemptive place without question. We don't question the fact that child
abuse has been practiced all around the world for centuries. As Breiner
(1990) notes, "We have been killing, maiming, and abusing our children for as long as our history has been recorded" (p. 1). Similarly,
Wilczynski's work (1997) notes that this systematic practice of child
killing has been conducted for "religious sacrifice, the culling of sick or
deformed infants, family planning, shame of illegitimacy, commerce
(in the form of 'baby farming') anger and mental disturbance" (p. 5).
Seeking to control childhood we only allow certain reports to surface
at certain times—those times when the masses are in need of subtle
reminders that our innocent children are not safe in the dark, cruel
world of childhood (Bray 1997; Leberg 1997).

A clear example of this occurred recently in Hawaii. On August 31,
1997, four-year-old Ruebyne Buentipo, was brought to the hospital in
a comatose state. Among his visual injuries were a severe skull frac-
ture, cigarette burns and bruises covering much of his body, and evidence of sexual abuse. On September 6, on the *Honolulu Advertiser's*
front page of the second section, the headline read, "Trial Ordered in
Case of 4-Year-Old in Coma." On September 11, another section B
headline stated, "State Errors Imperil Children." A few days later another headline read, "How Do We Guard Children?" After a brief period with no child abuse headlines (a period dominated by stories of
Princess Di's death), a period apparently in which the newspaper jour-
nalists busily researched background information to bolster their up-
coming stories, the media erupted with front-page headlines depicting
child abuse as a serious problem in Hawaii.

Suddenly coverage in the morning paper, the *Honolulu Advertiser*
was dominated by lead stories about child abuse, stories meant to give

the impression that child abuse in the state was increasing and, therefore, "produced a massive and intense coverage by the press, official and semi-official spokesmen" (Hall et alia 1978, p. 17). The moral panic was initiated with three bold, cover-story headlines in a four-day period. On October 21, the first headline stated, "State Failed To Protect 4-Year-Old"; on October 22, the title read, "Abuse Team Shocked When Boy Was Returned to Mother"; and on October 24, "3 Doctors Target Laws on Abuse" was the lead story. In the media's attempt to "etch child abuse on our collective conscience" (Wilczynski 1997) these articles dominated the week's news, speaking about the prevalence of child abuse in Hawaii, about how Hawaii's child protective services don't work, and a plea from the media for society to "do something about it" (save the children), before it happens again.

It is helpful here to analyze this moral panic using Goode and Ben-Yehuda's (1994) five central characteristics of the classic moral panic. Based on this analysis, first of all there is a greatly heightened level of concern. We see that in the review of the *Honolulu Advertiser* headlines, the way the media depicted child abuse here in Hawaii. Second, it involves increased hostility toward those associated with that activity. In this case, the mother of the boy, the presumably guilty party, almost assumed less guilt than the State's Child Protective Services, which allowed the boy to be returned to his mother even after five previous placements in foster care in his young life. Next, there is a high degree of consensus among society that the activity does represent a real and serious threat. Again, the media helped achieve this consensus (Brant and Too 1994), especially with headlines like "How Do We Guard Children?" Fourth, the nature of the threat is greatly exaggerated. This particular case, a tragic case indeed, is one of several millions cases of reported child abuse each year. In fact, each year somewhere between 1,200 to 1,300 children die because of child abuse injuries alone. Lastly, Goode and Ben-Yehuda note that moral panics are very volatile, as they subside almost as suddenly as they erupt. We've not witnessed much local media coverage of child abuse in the past several months, especially in comparison to the one week in October 1997 when three different page-one headlines dominated the news.

As Goode and Ben-Yehuda (1994) specified, during the moral panic, "serious steps must be taken to control the behavior, punish the perpetrators, and repair the damage . . . something must be done about it, and that something must be done now; if steps are not taken immediately . . . we will suffer even graver consequences" (p. 31). And so within weeks a new four-person child abuse police commission was appointed, lawmakers convened legislative task forces, set up to address the "problem" and as a whole Hawaii acted concerned (Leberg 1997). These steps are precisely what Hall et alia's (1978) work revealed, as they note, ". . . public concern is itself strongly shaped by the criminal statistics and the impression that there is 'wave after wave' of new kinds of crime" (p. 38).

Just this past week similar concerns were felt five thousand miles away in Massachusetts, as the nineteen-year-old English *au pair*, Louise Woodward, was convicted of murdering an eight-month-old baby boy in her care. Reports like the Woodward case are carefully chosen and shared by the media, so that the public always knows that adults are once again needed to serve and protect children (Alanen 1994), so that the larger bureaucracies (i.e., child protection services) stay in business, and so that "feel good" legislation provides us with an extra ounce of security practices (Freeman-Longo 1996). And so, several years ago when Polly Klass was kidnapped from her room in Petaluma, California, and then murdered by a drifter, *Newsweek* magazine ran a cover story entitled, "Kids Growing Up Scared" (subtitled "New Fears and Pressures Are Robbing a Generation of Its Childhood"). The feature article dialogue, now becoming more and more familiar, resonated,

> Something precious has gone out of American culture, and we don't know how to get it back . . . what we've lost goes beyond the fear of crime. It is the unspoken consensus that held children to be a privileged class deserving protection from adult concerns and responsibilities. Increasingly they are left to fend for themselves in a world of hostile strangers, and dangerous sexual enticements. (Adler 1994, p. 44)

And just three years later a related story from Ontario, Canada, reveals that we should still be worried about child abuse,

> A report painted a grim picture of society's treatment of young children . . . the study was based on nearly 10,000 interviews conducted in 1990–91 with subjects aged 15 and up. It found that almost one-third of males experienced physical abuse as children while 12.8 percent of females reported being subjected to some form of sexual abuse. (Maclean's 1997, p. 15)

Every year stories and statistics like these are released and marketed to the public as potential moral panics. In many of these irrational cases of moral panic, the public's response (and its ability to police) is much stronger than the facts justify (Howitt 1993; Johnson 1997). Cases like the rape and murder of seven-year-old Megan Kanka,

a crime committed by a known, convicted sex offender who was released from prison and lived across the street from her, are so emotionally volatile and socially anxiety-producing that they have the power
to quickly change our ways of being in the world (*Economist*, 1993),
especially through changes in the law (Fryer 1993). The Kanka case
produced a new federal legislative act, now known as Megan's Law,
which "requires registration and public notification of sex offenders
released into the community" (Freeman-Longo 1996, p. 96). "Feel
good" legislative acts like this encourage us to feel better on the surface, while little is known about the effects of this type of legislation
on reducing sexual abuse in the communities in which we live (Brinton
and Heinrich 1997; Gilbert 1991; Freeman-Longo 1996). And so we
are reminded, in stories like a recent one in a local paper, which note,

> The nation's courts are full of cases involving violent death, and no one ever
> hears about them. This episode struck a nerve for good reason: It was not so
> much about the circumstances surrounding the death of an infant as it was
> about the series of events that put the boy's life in the care of Louise Wood-
> ward. Americans are profoundly ambivalent about strangers raising their chil-
> dren. The Woodward case affirmed that national uncertainty. (Terzian 1997,
> p. A16)

Even though child abuse has been practiced all around the world
for centuries, situating this phenomenon in so-called safe places like
schools and child-care settings (e.g., where we now have McMartin
preschool-type accounts of child sex rings and ritualized child abuse),
has allowed for revisioning the construction and packaging of child
abuse. With this revisioning we now have *"expanded surveillance
[which] has, needless to say, revealed more intrusions into their
state of well-being"* (Jenks 1996, p. 108). This surveillance is evident in the growth and development narratives that so pervade popular parenting early childhood education literature. These accounts of
natural, nurturing, innocent children are then situated against other
accounts of children. In these other troubling accounts we hear about
adult teachers who sodomized children (e.g., "stuck an air tube up his
rectum . . . made the boy ride naked on a horse . . . pricked the boy's
finger and put it in a goat's anus . . . [Money 1995, p. 86]).

These unsettling, disturbing accounts allow us quite easily to retrieve the child's/our innocence and create a more modern genealogy
of what has come to count as "abuse.' in the new genealogy of child
abuse, the fictitious accounts ("he [the teacher] made the boy ride
naked on a horse . . . pricked the boy's finger and put it in a goat's

anus") are now quite believable, and instead of taking a risk of these things happening in our schools, child-care centers, and even our homes, we rule out even the remote possibility of these occurrences. As a result teachers are forced to keep their doors and window coverings open at all times, we've disallowed corporal punishment in schools, males are not allowed to change diapers in child-care settings, and parents have been arrested for taking pictures of their nude children.

Child Abuse

That child abuse is a critical problem of overwhelming proportion worldwide is a dramatic understatement. That this problem then should be thrust squarely on the shoulders of those who care for children a significant part of the day, teachers, is gross negligence. Taeuber's research reveals that between 1975 and 1991, the number of children being sexually abused in the United States nearly quadrupled (1991). In 1989 about 2.4 million American children, most under age five, were reported to have been physically, sexually, or mentally abused (Newman and Buka 1991). The United States 1991 census data reported that well over 430,000 children were reported to be sexual abuse victims (U.S. Bureau of the Census). Although no true consensus is reached on these precise figures (Melton and Flood 1994), most acknowledge that child sexual abuse is of major concern (McLeod and Wright 1996).

Even though child abuse remains an issue of solemn societal concern (Kelly, Brant, and Waterman 1993), research evidence reveals that there is no reason to single out early education settings as places where it is *likely* to happen. A 1986 study by the American Association for Protecting Children revealed that school personnel were involved in less than 1 percent of reported child sexual abuse cases nationwide (Nowesnick 1993). Sorenson's *Educational Administration Quarterly* article (1991) reported that there were six judicial cases dealing with school-related child abuse in 1987, ten in 1988, sixteen in 1989, and nineteen at the end of 1990, a total of fifty-one law-related decisions in a four-year period. Wells et alia's research (1995) reveals that the rate of child abuse in out-of-home settings is somewhere between 1 percent and 7 percent.

Yet, other reports single out school settings as vulnerable, at-risk places where "innocent" children should beware of potential abuse. For instance, Shakeshaft and Cohan's (1994) recent work reviews cases in which students were reportedly sexually abused by teachers or other professional staff, work that leads them to then propose that, ". . . children are at risk in schools and that some of the very people who are supposed to be helping them end up inflicting harm" (p. 43). In similar fashion, Fossey and DeMitchell's (1995) findings qualify them to state, "Sexual abuse against children is a continuing problem in the public schools. Although it is impossible to state the exact extent of the problem, recent studies show that it is not a rare phenomenon" (p. 3). Their report cites the 1993 American Association of University Women's survey that states that 25 percent of females in grades eight through eleven, and 10 percent of the males in that age group had been sexually molested in some way at school by an adult. In New York City, the recently released report of the Joint Commission of the Chancellor and the Special Commissioner discusses recommendations about "a child sexual abuse problem (in public schools) that is undeniably real" (Fossey and DeMitchell 1995, p. 2). Gilbert's review (1991) of fifteen different surveys conducted since 1976 illustrates disparate results, with one survey noting that 6 percent of women have been sexually abused during childhood, while another survey stated that the figure was 62 percent. Another important issue to consider here is the fact that the number of false reports of child abuse (alleged child abuse with no substantiation) swelled from 35 percent in 1976 to 65 percent in 1985 (Spiegel 1988). As Goode and Ben-Yehuda (1994) reveal, "In moral panics, the generation and dissemination of figures or numbers is extremely important—addicts, deaths, dollars, crimes, victims, injuries, illnesses—and most of the figures cited by moral panic 'claims-makers' are wildly exaggerated" (p. 36).

Reports like the abovementioned give the impression that child abuse in schools, particularly sexual abuse, is increasing while "producing a massive and intense coverage by the press, official and semi-official spokesmen" (Hall et alia 1978, p. 17). Yet, from what data we have on known cases of child sexual abuse in school settings, we have very little to no hard facts about its prevalence in educational settings in general (Nowesnick 1993). And if, as Fossey and DeMitchell argue, "It seems clear that school leaders can reasonably expect that a school child might be sexually abused by a school employee" (1995, p. 23), then based on the available statistical data compiled to date, couldn't we also argue that that same child "might be sexually abused" by a priest, a cop, a swimming teacher, or even more likely a mother, father, aunt, or uncle? In fact, reports like those mentioned above fail, in their zeal to point fingers at schools as dangerous places for children, to legitimate where child sexual abuse is most likely to occur—in the home (Boyle 1997).

As is evidenced by the statistical data collected to date, the overwhelming majority of acts of child abuse occur *within the family setting* (Conte and Fogarty 1990; Elrod and Rubin 1993; Finkelhor, Williams, and Burns, 1988). For instance, a 1996 U.S. Department of Health and Human Services Report revealed that child abuse perpetrators were parents or other relatives in 90 percent of reported cases. Trickett and Susman's research found that 87 percent of abusive incidents involved a parent or parent substitute (1988). In her review of the research, Bronwyn Mayden's notes, "In spite of a few highly publicized incidents and many urgent warnings about 'stranger danger,' 80% of all sexual assaults against children are committed by family members, friends, and acquaintances" (1996, p. 28). Similarly, a 1990 survey revealed that about 79 percent of child sexual abusers are related to the victims (Batchelor, et alia 1990).

Our growing concern about child sexual abuse (Berliner 1997) and the recognized profitable potential of curriculum design and school district adoption by the business community, has led to the creation and implementation of an abundance of educational intervention programs claiming to prevent abuse (Albers 1991; Berrick and Gilbert 1991; deYoung 1988; Hollander 1992). Tharinger et alia (1988) estimate that four hundred to five hundred child abuse prevention curricula have been designed for and implemented in schools and other social service settings. Even though millions of dollars have been funneled into school-based interventions, and millions of young children have participated in these prevention curricula, we know little about *the* most effective ways to prevent or ameliorate the problem (Lumsden 1992; McEvoy 1990; Skibinski 1995). In fact, statistical data show few outcome effects of these various interventions (Bogat and McGrath 1993; Conte and Fogarty 1990; Daro 1991; Krivacska 1989).

Although mostly well-intentioned child advocates helped witness the increase of sexual abuse prevention programs, much of the evaluative data on prevention curricula reveal that these school-based programs are simply inappropriate, especially those geared for young children. Typically the conceptual knowledge these programs hope to teach includes: as a child you own your own body; discerning the range of touches on the touch (recognizing different kinds of touches, from "good" to "bad"); secrets about touching can and should be told;

children have a range of responsible adults they can go to for support while revealing touching problems; and how to say "No!" to an offending person and getting away from them (Borkin and Frank 1986; Conte and Fogarty 1990; Conte, Rosen and Saperstein 1986; deYoung 1988; McLeod and Wright 1996).

Among the concerns about the inappropriateness of many of these programs for young children, specialists note that certain curricula "have the potential for creating a distorted view of sexuality in children's minds" (Lumsden 1992, p. 44). Gilbert (1988) questions how a four-year-old child who cannot understand Piaget's laws of conservation can "understand lessons that try to convey the far more subtle change of emotions . . . aroused by a soft touch that at first feels good, then becomes confusing, and finally feels bad" (p. 6). McEvoy (1990) notes that curricula that "emphasize 'good' or 'bad' touch may run the risk of confusing young children, generating fear or anxiety in them, causing children to reject appropriate displays of parental affection, and increase conflicts between schools and parents over sex education" (p. 256).

Gilbert goes on to point out that we are asking too much when we: require children to identify the difference between a "red flag" and a "green flag" touch; teach about private parts with wide-ranging definitions of which body parts are private and which are not; and, teach that any physical touch that does not feel good is a "bad touch." Some curriculum models identify that a "parent's affectionate pat on the behind of a four-year-old may appear as an act that violates the dictum against touching private parts, or as one to be consciously appraised by the child to determine its goodness or badness" (p. 14).

It is disturbing to think about what the "no touch" moral panic has done to those we are supposed to serve. As Gilbert writes (1988):

> Preschool children need care and security. At a time in their lives when it is important for them to feel that their parents will nurture and protect them, should children be taught that they must evaluate the boundaries of appropriate adult behavior? The underlying message in the "empowerment" of four-year-olds is that they must try to control the dangerous outside world. It is an abdication of family and community responsibility—a sorry message for our times.
>
> Real dangers do, of course, exist. A distressing number of children are at risk of physical and emotional injury from adults whose touches are not innocent expressions of affection. To criticize sexual abuse prevention training for preschoolers is not to deny the serious problems these programs hope to alleviate. However, "empowering" four-year-olds, whom we normally forbid to cross the street alone, defies common sense. At best, it is a social placebo

that may only bewilder small children while soothing parental anxieties; at worst, it leaves youngsters as vulnerable as ever but psychologically on edge— a little more aware of the dangers around them and a little less able to enjoy the innocence of childhood. (p. 14)

From an evaluation standpoint these "one size fits all" programs (McLeod and Wright 1996) continue to be designed and implemented based on unstudied and unchallenged assumptions about children's understanding of sexual abuse prevention. What we do ultimately, in our zeal to protect children, is "create popular and fun presentations that grab the attention and the enthusiasm of children, but ultimately [we] still leave them at risk for sexual abuse" (deYoung 1988, p. 67).

Even those who advocate that we actively teach against "no touch" cower down to the panic as the supposed advocacy position they occupy does very little to fight the moral panic. For instance, Del Prete (1997) begins a recent article noting that in the past several years more and more schools have forced teachers to abstain from touching students in their care, and then proactively reminds the reader that "not touching children could be considered another form of abuse— neglect" (p. 59). Yet near the end of this narrative Del Prete asks teachers to follow these suggested guidelines when considering touch in the classroom: (1) Consider the age, sex, and perception (maturity) of the child; (2) Use touch only to praise or comfort; (3) Ensure there is another adult present; and (4) Briefly touch only the shoulder or arm (1997). So while presuming trying to take a stance against "no touch" this article buckles under the moral panic and readily accepts "no touch" policy.

Conclusions

Even though we've gone to great lengths to burden prospective teachers with background fingerprinting and credential checks, and probationary surveillance periods, it seems we still don't really trust all of these protective procedures. Why is it that after implementing all these different security measures we still don't trust ourselves, so even after the relentless background checks we continue incorporating rigid policies, like Australia's "Child Care and Mobile Children's Services Regulations" which state, "Two staff are to be present at any one time to protect and supervise children" (Bryson 1996). Similarly, many centers now incorporate and enforce policies that demand that at least two teachers be in the diaper changing area during every diaper change.

Many other centers don't let males change diapers at all! What is the reasoning behind the checks? Shouldn't the thorough review of all of the required staff background documents help employers rest easy and then reveal to administrators that he is a good diaper changer and could do so without supervision or that she was able to take supervisorial charge and oversee the bathroom area on her own?

We allow "no touch" to name itself via pictures of missing children on milk cartons, via newspaper and magazine cover stories, via books and movie specials, puppet shows, lectures, and even via traveling actors (Spiegel 1988; Tobin 1997). In his study of moral panic Jenkins (1992) notes that this ". . . act of naming a thing gives a person symbolic control over it" (p. 2). Thus is the case of "no touch" as now it has been named, controlled, and marketed as a moral panic. The creative marketing of this moral panic by the dominant social order insists that child abuse is made overly familiar to us all and not by "coinage of a simple term but by transmitting child abuse as part of a whole context of troubling themes and images" (Hall et alia 1978). So troubling indeed, that teachers and other child service providers have allowed it to define how they physically interact with those children in their care (Duncan 1998). We have allowed the naming of child abuse as a societal-wide problem to be more narrowly applied to our immediate work, as a child-caregiver/teacher problem. We have allowed ourselves to be named us as potential abusers, unless we incorporate "no touch" policies to protect ourselves and those children in our care. We have allowed childhood to be named as innocence and so we work hard to protect that.

Chapter 3

Strange Stories of Surveillance

> . . . it is always the body that is at issue—the body and its forces, their utility and their docility, their distribution and their submission.
> —Michel Foucault, *Discipline and Punish: The Birth of the Prison*

> . . . influenced and pressurized by a harsh new climate of decisiveness and urgency, in which risk was not to be tolerated, [we] increasingly became like police officers and surveillance operators. . . . childcare workers during that period can recall the ceaseless flow of 'urgent' memos and updates of procedures quickly following on the publication of each report.
> —Kieran O'Hagan and Karola Dillenburger, *The Abuse of Women within Childcare Work*

Following from the previous discussion on moral panic, this chapter draws on a collection of narratives from the field, candidly revealing how prevalent the moral panic of "no touch" is, as it has clearly entered both professional (classroom) and personal (home) contexts (e.g., a father who questions his parenting abilities—"Did I inappropriately touch her vagina when I changed her diaper?"—and anecdotal reports of fathers in New South Wales who won't bathe their own child(ren) after the release of the Paedophile Index in that Australian state).

In her recent work, Thompson suggests that, "Some things one can see for oneself. Other things depend on the telling of the tale" (1998, p. 537). Numerous caregiver narratives were perused to help portrait the widespread prevalence of "no touch." To assist in this illustrative process, an extensive presentation of "no touch" stories is offered here. While these examples are similar in form to the several introductory narrative cases presented in the first chapter, they are meant to build on those earlier samples, revealing in quantity and quality, just how pervasive "no touch" has become.

After first presenting a collection of "no touch" teacher stories this chapter then interrogates the thematic undertones of that narrative content, especially in relation to moral panic. Then other related stories, interpretations, analyses, and images (Turner and Sparrow 1997) of "no touch" will be interrogated, including professional literature advocating for "no touch."

I chose to represent "no touch" through the telling of stories, given that, "the story has become recognized as one of the central roots we have into the continuing quest for understanding human meaning . . . indeed culture itself has been identified as an ensemble of stories we tell about ourselves" (Plummer 1995, p. 5). Dilg notes that "reading and listening to each other's stories . . . give us tools for survival in this multicultural nation" (1997, p. 64). Stories allow us to (re)capture the past and make new meanings of life events (Slunt 1994). The "no touch" stories are offered here as a collection of narratives representing a collective group of people, an "interpretive community" (Fish 1980) who care for children in out-of-home settings. In this particular instance this interpretive community consists of teachers, child-care workers, future caregivers (students who are studying to be teachers), and in several cases mothers and fathers. This interpretive community tells and retells stories, offering their own interpretations of "no touch." In this sense the people whose stories are shared here are acting as "interpreters . . . as extensions of an institutional community" (Fish 1980, p. 321).

Like the interpretive community represented here, I too am attempting to interpret "no touch" by presenting it, first in literal translations from the original teachers' transcripts, and then re-presenting it back to the group of teachers who speak here and ultimately to all the other teachers whose voices were not textualized in this book. In the quest to further interrogate "no touch" and as a function of interpretation (Fish 1980), these stories will be retold by others. The stories will shift, and as Plummer notes (1995):

> . . . no stories are true for all time and space: We invent our stories with a passion, they are momentarily true, we may cling to them, they may become our lives and then we may move on. Clinging to the story, changing the story, reworking it, denying it. But somewhere behind all this story telling there are real active, embodied, impassioned lives. (p. 170)

One reason I'm writing this book, one reason I chose to interpret, why I chose to tell a story, was because I too wanted to speak to the many thousands of "active, embodied, impassioned lives" that are operating within and around the multiple discourses of "no touch."

As caregivers of young children, I wanted these lives, all of which are "suspended in webs of significance they themselves have spun" (Brettell 1993, p. 2), to consider again and again the impact of "no touch" on their daily existence.

The intent here, then, is to express a history we can all fit into ("case history with holes"), so that all those who are part of "no touch" "are ourselves inserted into it (the case history) without even minimal distance" (Jameson 1986). While reading and considering these "no touch" narratives, hopefully the reader will embed herself/himself into the history, whether or not she/he feels an intimate part of "no touch." By witnessing our experience as a "case history with holes," "What is made possible is the experience of something for the first time that at the same time seems to be already known, known before . . . Thus certain narrative elements are intensified so that their historical sense makes itself felt" (Clough 1992, p. 125). By drawing on a wide variety of different stories, different "cultural resources" (Moss 1993), the reader will further shape and reshape the story into different kinds of "no touch" stories.

The bulk of this chapter represents narrative threads from stories that were shared on two electronic list servers, KIDSPHERE and ECENET. These stories reflect running commentary initiated by a caregivers, preservice teachers, parents, and teachers, all of which was posted in response to the National Public Radio program, "Day Care Center Goes to Extreme to Protect Reputation". NPR broadcast this a story of a day-care center that implemented staff policies that constrained staff from touching the children in their care (see the appendix for the complete NPR transcript). Note that while this particular "no touch" story initially triggered the list serve commentary, much of this commentary went well beyond that story. So even though the NPR story was surprising news to some, many other teacher respondents have been participating in a "no touch" world for many years.

List Serve (KIDSPHERE and ECENET) Stories from the Field

While the original "no touch" list serve dialogue was quite extensive, covering a wide range of topics, this section includes only the thematic content gleaned from these list serve postings that closely relates to issues presented in chapters 1 and 2. The common themes that were woven throughout much of the list serve thread include: caregiver fear of accusations; how to touch children; effect of "no touch" on our collective conscience; and perceptions of how to professionally "be" with those in our care. Note that in each of the following thematic passages the verbatim respondent commentary is identified as italicized text, with each new response indented.

Caregiver Fear of Accusations

Many respondents revealed the overwhelming fear they have of touching children in their care. Dialogue on the list serve thread was dominated by a language of fear (e.g., "This is very scary stuff," "Take precautions," "Never get yourself into the position," and "Abuse scenarios are always on my mind"). Representative list serve commentary which supports this caregiver fear includes several comments from male teachers, such as:

> As a result of my fear I do not touch students, except maybe on the shoulder or arm, and I do not show any affect except verbally unless initiated by the student first.

Another male teacher shares:

> This is very scary stuff. I think we have all heard horror stories concerning false accusations made by students against teachers. As a male teacher (27 years) I have thought about this a zillion times. The way things are, men in particular must be extremely cautious.

In the next example, a male teacher informs the list serve audience:

> A third-grade girl in my room told her parents I had walked in on her while she was in the restroom and "watched" her. As one might imagine they were at the classroom door in the morning. Nothing came of it as I was teaming with a lady who came to my assistance. She informed the parents that I never went into the girls' restroom just as she never entered the boys' restroom. Ended up the parents were talking divorce and the child had used this to try to get them back together. BUT, my career came very close to being greatly harmed or ruined.

Another male shares:

> Yes, abuse scenarios are always on the mind (though they never, and never should, dominate or control my actions).

Several "new" male teachers who just completed their teacher preparation program, share:

> Men can do more than change diapers. But with the way society is right now you are giving them plenty of reasons not to come anywhere near this line of work.

and,

> *This issue really scares the hell out of me and I often wonder how far reaching the implications of withdrawal of affection may go.*

Similarly, one other novice teacher warns:

> *Never get yourself into the position of having your moral integrity questioned! Once an accusation is made it sticks regardless of whether you have done something wrong or not.*

Several veteran teachers expressed their concerns in the following ways:

> *The people who have some of the biggest impact on children's lives, their teachers, are scared to death to do some little things to change how boys are constructed. They must continue to keep their distance, appear to be cold and emotionless, etc., etc., all of which simply reinforces all that is negative about stereotyped 'maleness' and which allows men to do the violence they do because they have become so desensitized to warm feelings and touching.*

and,

> *From a statistical point of view, the risk is minuscule . . . teaching is a very safe profession. But we don't let the fear of disaster immobilize us: we take sensible precautions, and then live our lives . . . most of us very well. For me, I always took the simple precaution of never being alone with a child.*

In the last few examples several parents revealed their concerns about "no touch" issues:

> *Now we have a highly qualified man who will probably be turned down for a job because of the hysteria that our directionless society has created. We began to create this phenomena of men molesting children when we began to remove men from our households and started giving them the very strong message that they were no longer needed or wanted.*

and,

> *They are so afraid of being accused of child abuse they have on their own adopted a "hands off" policy. As a note, what may have prompted this is recently a kindergarten teacher has been charged with child abuse. He has not been in court yet, but probably even if he is found innocent his career has been ruined. Because of a few bad apples everyone must suffer.*

How to Touch Children

Again and again, list serve respondents expressed personal concerns they have about how to/not to touch children in their care. Referring to the local media one teacher respondent was informed, *"DON'T EVER TOUCH A CHILD—If you are a male."* Another woman shared:

> Just yesterday I read in our local paper that our elementary school teachers are no longer hugging or touching their students. A male teacher will request a teacher's aid or parent to be with him in the classroom if a female student will be alone with him. They will also take along another adult if they must help a child in the bathroom.

By employing physical *("As a male I always have to keep at arms length")* and emotional (*"Abandon the idea of showing affection"*) distancing tactics, many teachers readily personalize "no touch" as part of their own teaching practices. Many teachers are quite willing to simply not touch any of the children in their care (*"With body contact I avoid it. A teacher in the school a while back was accused of sexual harassment after he touched a female student on the shoulder,"* and *"I never touch a child, personal choice. I do not touch any child and many of my students are having hugging withdrawals. During the first three weeks of school, nearly every student asked why I would not hug them. I responded that it was a personal choice, and explained that I never touch them, including not patting them on the back or arm").* For many of those teachers who are willing to touch, they do so only by following certain strict guidelines (*"I haven't totally abandoned the idea of showing affection, however, I do all of my hugging, arm touching, head patting in very public places with lots of other children and adults present,"* and *"I will let the kids hug me or hold my hand, etc., but I make it very clear who is doing the touching,"* and *"I am very careful to never touch a child when no one else is around (and certainly only touch them on their shoulder or arm)."*

Effects of "No Touch" on Our Collective Conscience

The list serve commentary illustrates that much of the thinking goes well beyond simple surface level formulae about "how to" interact with children, as respondents shared that many of the "no touch" issues have entered deeply into our collective psyche. Teachers expressed that "no touch" has compelled them and all of society to consider teacher subjectivity and the construction of teacher identities as the "other" (*"Many people have brought up the notion that men working with young children are somehow not quite normal. Either they are gay, recluses, or some sort of closet pedophile—or so the stereotype goes"; "There is considerable blurring of the lines that define normal and abnormal sexual behavior"; "'No touch' scares me because as you all probably know, elementary students like to hug teachers, like affection, and do not want to be treated like they have some dreadful disease"*).

Many respondents report that they are constantly thinking about "no touch" issues. This is readily evident in commentary like, *"I am very aware of showing any affection (physical or verbal) to children, and often I find myself wanting to give them a hug or supportive measure, but unable to because the DANGER/CAUTION sign is always flashing in the back of my mind,"* or *"Recently, while on practicum a young boy came up to me and gave me a hug. I just froze, my mind was racing at a million miles an hour. Do I hug him back? If I do is that taken the student-teacher relationship too far? Why shouldn't I be able to give him a hug? Why should I be even having to think all this stuff?"*

Similarly, other teachers shared, *"I have thought about this a zillion times. It seems totally unfair that the female teachers can always hug their students, some getting hugs by every student every day as they board the bus,"* and, *"Fear of abuse accusations is such a domineering sentiment that it governs and restricts our capacity for caring for our young wards. As a male in the field I am bombarded almost daily with questions on these topics."* The last related comments include, *"It saddens me to have to think twice before putting a bandage on a child's elbow because I CARE, and I happen to be a man. We need people who are willing to challenge societies discrimination, and teach because you want to and you care. I would however, take on all of the suggestions of the others such as, keeping your classroom door open as much as possible, not allowing yourself to be alone with a child, and making sure other adults are within the school building."*

The far-reaching effects of "no touch" go beyond classroom teachers, as parents also consider quality child care through the lenses of "no touch," as the following cases exhibit. In the first example a mother shares:

> *The idea of child abuse for that center has never even crossed my mind. Every room has several windows, more than one teacher and a video cam-*

era which is hooked to two monitors in the director's office so that rooms can be observed at any time. I used these when I first brought my son there. I was so apprehensive about leaving him the director invited me to stay in her office and watch him on the monitor until I felt comfortable enough to leave him.

In the last example an administrator shares:

Parents were OK with this but a few were pretty uncomfortable at first . . . and insisted that we re-think our hiring of a male. We have had a couple of parents who have pulled their children out. It's too bad, but there is bias towards men in the field.

How to Professionally "Be" with Those in Our Care

Much like the previous thematic commentary, here we see that these list serve respondents were using "no touch" to professionally position themselves within their work with children. Just as the teachers in earlier accounts expressed an underlying fear about "no touch" issues, teacher respondents here also expressed the need to always be on guard in the classroom ("*One has to be careful these days. It is unfortunate. This advice has worked for me. Do not initiate affection*"; "*Not being alone with students is a good rule of thumb. Discussing sensitive issues is also better done with a partner present. I don't like it, but that's the way it is*"; "*I am an ECE major and plan to teach in the early grades, but having to put my career on the line day in and day out has given me something to think about*"; "*I am, however, also aware of the close line between welcoming hugs and wrong attention and am always careful never to touch a child first, and always to make the contact brief*").

Respondents reveal that they are constructing their teacher subjectivity with a heavy influence from "no touch," as they express:

In the school where I work I have been told by female teachers that I often appear to be cold and uncaring towards students but with all the court appearances who can blame me. I do show some verbal emotion toward students but only if there is another teacher or student/s in the room.

Another teacher shares:

Children need the gift of touch, they need to feel wanted and most of all they need to feel valued. But I'm male and part of my teaching code prevents me from showing the care that I often want to show. I often think, do I really want to be that sort of teacher that the judicial system is (almost) forcing upon me?

In the last example here a teacher shares:

In response to your question about male teachers and female students I personally follow a few simple rules that were passed on to me: Never be in a room alone; Never close the door if you are alone; Never touch or ask inappropriate questions; Never say things that can be misconstrued; Treat your students how you would want your children treated if you were their teacher.

Like many of the issues in chapter 2, teachers here refer to "moral panic" examples that have influenced their practices:

Several years ago, some lovely little girls decided to get their teacher and told someone he kissed them on the cheek and one girl said he rubbed her leg. The whole thing was awful, it was during the time of all the hysteria over child abuse, the investigation was carried out by some very stupid people who decided that when they asked if something made a kid feel uncomfortable it equaled sex. The legal fees alone were over $120,000. It was so bad that no teacher would agree to be interviewed by the authorities without their lawyer present and a tape recorder. The jury reached a verdict of not guilty in about 1 hour. The teacher received all back pay. The tax payers got zonked all the way around by incompetent investigators. And you want to know why teachers in my school are afraid to hug a kid?

While studying "no touch" I came upon and read many list serve postings like, "*I am lucky to have always had a female aide to balance our 'team'. She seems to have a very nice way of meeting the children's needs but has some little mannerisms that I would not or could not use. Combing or brushing a little girl's hair, straightening clothes, putting in hair clips, looking at scrapes under tights, etc. I really do not encourage sitting in laps or picking children up.*" As this passage denotes, clearly differentiated, gendered teaching practices present themselves throughout the "no touch" list serve thread. In other similar examples, teachers share comments like:

Women teachers are expected to show warmth and hug their students; men are expected to be distant and 'model' that this is what it is to be man and as a result are wondering about being involved at all.

Or,

I was not hired because the director did not want me working there because I am a male, and she was afraid of what I would do to the children. I became angry and hurt. So, even if you don't do anything, guys, you still may be discriminated against simply because you don't fit the male sex role stereotype.

Another respondent offers:

When I was teaching preschool we hired an incredibly great guy to be my assistant teacher with the three-year-olds. He was intelligent, fun and genuinely loved the kids. Most of the parents were OK with this but a few were pretty uncomfortable at first. One mother came and told us that her daughter was terrified of men (other than her father) and insisted that we re-think our hiring of him. In fact, her daughter took to this teacher just as quickly as the other children.

In a related example, a teacher asked list serve users to consider this:

I would like to solicit some points-of-view on a situation that is happening at my daughter's preschool for 2 1/2–5 year olds. Currently, both morn-ing teachers for my daughter's group (younger) are women, while one of the afternoon teachers is a man and the other a woman. Recently, the female afternoon teacher left for another position. There is a candidate for her position who seems to be well-qualified, and who happens also to be a man. However, there is a sense among some involved with the center, that it would be inadvisable to have both afternoon teachers be men.

The last example from a male teacher:

I am still reflecting on the previous post that said, 'The man should not help out with bathroom chores.' Come on, it seems like every other picture I see of a man and a child he is changing their diaper. Therefore, being a man majoring in this field really upsets me.

Finally, a parent expresses her thoughts on "no touch":

Truly sad. Some of my boy's (I also have three) best teachers were males in elementary grades. I truly feel for their "predicament" since I KNOW they are truly sensitive, intelligent human beings—but they are also MALE— this "guilty until proven innocent" attitude is not doing a great service to our children. I believe the loss is greater from the abandonment of male elementary grade teachers from our system than the possible damage by "sexual abuse" which might occur in a few isolated cases.

Other "No Touch" Themes

As mentioned in the introduction to this chapter, the narratives pre-sented here are meant to draw on the previous discussion of moral panic and "no touch" as the phenomena are evidenced in the field of early childhood education. Although these particular narratives represent only a small sample of teacher perspectives from a particular source (i.e., the KIDSPHERE and ECENET electronic list servers), the commonalities these narratives share soon appear evident. These stories and other's like them speak to an issue of great importance—our (in)ability to freely be with those children in our care. While further reviewing the numerous narratives several other common themes appeared, which are furthered explored below.

Visibility, Surveillance and the Gaze

Even while scholars like Peggy Phelan note that increased visibility "summons surveillance and the law; it provokes voyeurism, fetishism, and the colonialist/imperial appetite for possession" (1993, p. 6), many of the respondents discussed common practices revealing their complicity in these policing practices (Watney 1987). These are caregiver practices that lead them to always remain visible, under surveillance, and under the gaze and guard of a larger, ever-watchful society.

This gaze is not unlike that which Michel Foucault discussed in his much publicized work, *Discipline and Punish* (1977). In this book Foucault discusses forms of social control that are achieved through the ideal of the Panopticon, the model prison which allows a prison supervisor to effortlessly watch, or gaze at each prisoner (society) from a central tower. Referring to Foucault, Pratt (1997) argues:

> Life in the panopticon would then be a kind of micro-society that was totally controlled and regulated—a version in miniature of the way society at large could be disciplined in the same way . . . the Panopticon became, according to Foucault, the model for the subsequent development of social control in modern society as a whole. On the one hand, we find strategies of discipline designed to produce 'the obedient subject, the individual subjected to habits, rules, orders, an authority that is exercised continually around him and upon him, and which he must allow to function automatically in him' (Foucault 1977: 128–9), ultimately leading to a transformation of 'the soul.' (p. 463)

While much of the "no touch" policing appears to be social control from without, many personal responses illustrated that self-policing of one's own subjectivity is also common for practitioners (Rose 1990). For as Foucault so keenly noted, "the inmate must never know whether he is being looked at any one moment, but he must be sure that he may always be so" (1977, p. 201). Some of the related caregiver responses reveal that many teachers are told to never cover up the window(s) on the classroom door and to keep the classroom door open as much as possible (e.g., "*I always leave the classroom door open,*" and "*I do all of my hugging, arm touching, head patting in very public places with lots of other children and adults present*"). Several other respondents revealed that they would *never* allow themselves to be alone with a student, expressing: "*I avoid being alone with a single child,*" and "*I'm also never alone with a student.*" Another teacher claimed, "*I have been told by female teachers that I often appear to be cold and uncaring towards students but with all the court appearances who can blame me? I do show some verbal emotion toward students but only if there is another teacher or student/s in the room. With body contact I avoid it.*" In another case a parent said that, "*The idea of child abuse for that center has never even crossed my mind. Every room has several windows, more than one teacher and a video camera which is hooked to two monitors in the director's office so that rooms can be observed at any time.*" Even though she says child abuse "never crossed her mind" this mom seems very secure in the knowledge that her son is constantly under video surveillance, an ever-watchful gaze!

Several of the teachers said that they are engaged in questioning their own moral integrity as they personalize "no touch" (e.g., "*Never get yourself into the position of having your moral integrity questioned!*" or "*I was mindful of the importance of preventing misunderstandings or even the appearance of impropriety. My policy was to never be alone with a child in a room, and to always conduct myself in an irreproachable manner.*"). And yet, "no touch" seems to control teacher practices (again this self-policing) more than teachers control or act against "no touch." This is vividly apparent in the following comments, whereby a female teacher advocates for all male teachers to keep up the good work (i.e., "*To all of the men out there . . . we need people who are willing to challenge societies discrimination, and teach because you want to and you care*"), then in the same breath she abruptly warns the men to reclaim the more safe "no touch" practices (i.e., "*I would however, take on all of the suggestions of the others such as, keeping your classroom door open as much as possible, not allowing yourself to be alone with a child, and making sure other adults are within the school building*").

These thematic comments disclose how teachers visualize themselves and their professional practices through the lenses of visibility and surveillance/gaze. As Rose (1990) notes, the very "soul of the citizen has entered directly into political discourse and the practice of government . . . government and parties of all political complexions have formulated policies, set up machinery, established bureaucracies and promoted initiatives to regulate the conduct of citizens by acting upon their mental capacities and propensities" (p. 2). That these notions of visibility and surveillance are both self-imposed and constructed by larger social conditions is evident as these teacher narratives hark back to the earlier discussion of the social control of moral panics.

Influence of 'No Touch' on Pedagogical Practices

Much of the narrative content speaks to critical pedagogical issues (e.g., *"Having to put my career on the line day in and day out"*) that impact the daily teaching practices of these particular teacher respondents and the larger teaching profession. "No touch" has far-reaching implications for what a teacher feels she/he can and can't do as a pedagogue. The following examples note that teachers are clearly making informed, conscientious decisions to refuse allowing touch to enter their teaching practices. First a teacher exclaims, *"I do not show any affect except verbally unless initiated by the student first."* Another teacher shares, *"Kids do run up and give me hugs and expect me to come to their rescue when they are upset. Floods of them meet me on the playground and say hello but I do not open my arms and encourage them to do hugging."* Still, other teachers report, *"I avoid hugging as much as possible—I assume the field goal stance—arms in air, body rigid, and absolutely no warmth or compassion,"* and *"This advice has worked for me. Do not initiate affection,"* or *"I am very aware of showing any affection (physical or verbal) to children, and often I find myself wanting to give them a hug or supportive measure, but unable to because the DANGER/ CAUTION sign is always flashing in the back of my mind."*

Even teachers-to-be, those preservice teachers who have not yet been formally indoctrinated into the profession, proclaim their acceptance of "no touch" as expressed through words like, *"I am an ECE major and plan to teach in the early grades, but having to put my career on the line day in and day out has given me something to think about"* and *"Recently, while on practicum a young boy came up to me and gave me a hug. I just froze, my mind was racing at a million miles an hour. Do I hug him back? If I do is that taking the student-teacher relationship too far?"*

While several teachers did seem to problematize "no touch" and the implications of that policy on their professional practices (e.g., *"One little kindergarten boy had just had it. He ran to me in tears and fell into my arms. He was tired and he needed comfort. What was I to do? Pat him on the head? I held him, took him for a walk to the office, and to the water fountain*") the majority of these teacher narratives reveal a profession that appears to have accepted "no touch" as a given part of their pedagogical practices (e.g., "*In the school where I work I have been told by female teachers that I often appear to be cold and uncaring towards students but with all the court appearances who can blame me*" and "*I never touch a child, personal choice. I do not touch any child and many of my students are having hugging withdrawals*").

Feminization and the Care of Young Children

While several male respondents were angered that they couldn't rightfully partake in classroom practices that their female counterparts could (e.g., "*It seems totally unfair that the female teachers can always hug their students, some getting hugs by every student every day as they board the bus. However, as a male teacher, I always have to keep at arms length*"), most of the respondents accepted their defined gendered teaching roles without question (e.g., "*If there are problems in clothing-sensitive areas—such as one day when I had to help a kindergartner with his belt buckle and pants zipper in the classroom—elicit the help of a fellow teacher, preferably a woman,*" and "*I have taught kindergarten for two years and am now teaching first grade. While in kinder, my assistant was female and she gave all the hugs that were given in our class. I was aware, as were parents of our students, that Mrs. 'D' hugged and I did not*"). These findings closely corroborate Witz, Halford, and Savage's work (1996), illustrating how people participate "daily in hierarchies that are visibly gendered . . . [and which] can be understood not simply as ordered spaces between jobs, but also spaces between bodies" (p. 188).

Early childhood education is a feminized field with the overwhelming majority of the professional and para-professional teacher corps dominated by females (O'Hagan and Dillenburger 1995). Yet, in our haste to initiate and follow "no touch" policies it seems we've allowed the very persons, women, who have, for better or worse, historically been constructed as nurturant, "motherlike" caregivers, to be quickly (re)constructed as potentially dangerous abusers. We see this (re)construction at work when re-examining some of the male teacher responses, like, "*Anytime a student has a problem which may be sensitive, I find a female teacher (regardless of the child's sex) to assist me, so that a witness is there,"* or *"I am lucky to have always had a female aide to balance our 'team'. She seems to have a very nice way of meeting the children's needs but has some little mannerisms that I would not or could not use (e.g., Combing or brushing a little girl's hair, straightening clothes, putting in hair clips, looking at scrapes under tights, etc.")*. Lastly, one other male said, *"If all they (children) run into is females that would be doing them quite a disservice."*

According to the teaching profession, women can touch, men can't. These narratives illustrate that the gendered role of the female caregiver/teacher is unproblematically defined as a person who can hug, a person who is *sensitive*, a person who is *very nice*, and a person who has unique skills (e.g., *"combing a little girl's hair, straightening clothes, putting in hair clips, looking at scrapes under tights"*). Just as unproblematically men are presented and constructed as persons who can't hug, persons who are insensitive, persons who are *not as nice*, and persons also possessing different, unique skills (e.g., *"good role models for little boys"; "because so few males are in ECE, the few that are MUST be good"; "they exhibit unique sexual roles as gays, recluses, or pedophiles"*). Even while feminism has been highly influential in alerting the public to the prevalence of child abuse (through sexually abused women's testimonies), feminist theory has had has little impact in early childhood education (O'Hagan and Dillenburger 1995).

Conclusions

Just a few years ago when I mentioned "no touch" to my colleagues and friends it was quickly laughed at and written off as "impossible," and yet it is now becoming more and more common in schools. I offer this collection of "no touch" stories to help us "rediscover our 'disremembered' past, a history . . . we have chosen to forget" (Dilg 1997, p. 64). Last year when I talked to parent and caregiver/teacher audiences in Australia the very first response I heard was, "Only in America!" Every response in every audience after that was, "Oh yeah, I work(ed) in a center where that ("no touch") is/was a policy." This policy, sometimes written, mostly unwritten, is affecting children, parents, teachers, social workers, child-care workers in various ways. If we can critically engage the many "no touch" stories that these caregivers and teachers and parents share as, "the pathways to understanding culture . . . the bases of identity . . . the tropes for making sense of the past . . . narrative truths for analysis" (Plummer 1995, p. 18), then maybe there is some hope that we can work against these policies and regain a sense of calm in our respective "child concern" disciplines.

Chapter 4

Strange Stories of Desire

Touch is important; we know that as human beings, in order to thrive, we need to be touched.
—Ros Hunt, *"Seventy Times Seven? Forgiveness and Sexual Violence in Christian Pastoral Care"*

Locating desire as the shape our dreams and identities take in the social, it becomes possible to speculate how it is that desire can work against and in our best interests.
—Ursula Kelly, *Schooling Desire: Literacy, Cultural Politics, and Pedagogy*

Working in direct opposition to the prior discussion of social control, this chapter illustrates that many teachers and researchers are actively working against the moral panic of "no touch," attempting to counter its potential negative effect in their classrooms and in society. Drawing again on narrative examples, this chapter begins by critiquing touch and teacher desire(s). Then I interrogate narratives from a small group of teachers who strongly advocate the inclusion of touch in their daily caregiving practices. Moving beyond personal teacher narratives, I then share one other example of a collective of touch advocates, researchers who are studying the benefits of touch at the Touch Research Institute in Miami, Florida.

Teacher Desire

One of the main reasons I went into early education as an undergraduate student is because I wanted to *be* with children, and to *be* with them in many ways, including emotionally, socially, and physically. Reflecting on this, desire leaps out at me as a word that helps me think of the ways I wanted to be with children. I've always enjoyed being with young children and to be able to get a degree that allowed me to get paid for doing that was a wonderful thought. I believe, like me, that teachers today have a longing, a desire to be with children, one of the main reasons they are teaching/caregiving in the early years. Several respondents spoke to this issue of desire in their "no touch" narratives. For example, one teacher said, "*Men can do more than change diapers. When I get my degree I will be able to prove that at least to a small percentage of people . . . that there are indeed effective, caring, loving males that could really impact the field of education.*"

Another teacher shared, "*One little boy had just had it. He ran to me in tears and fell into my arms. He was tired and he needed comfort. What was I to do? Pat him on the head? I held him, took him for a walk to the office . . . to the water fountain. We returned to the group. He was fine after that. Children need a hug some-times.*" The next teacher, a male, lamented ". . . *it seems totally unfair that the female teachers can always hug their students, some getting hugs by every student every day. However, as a male teacher, I always have to keep at arms length.*"

Several more teachers spoke of desire when they considered their ways of being with young children. In the next case a woman shares, "*I refuse to let the ugly specter of fingerpointing be a chokechain. I smile and I wink at my children. I hug and tickle my children. I give praise and encouragement where and when it is due. Being confident and secure that my actions and intentions are rooted in caring and nurturing I shall continue to be this way.*" In the next case a male reveals that, "*I have been known to carry someone back to the nurse's office, even if they could have walked. I believe this gives the child much more comfort and relief.*" Lastly, in the follow-ing case I believe it was desire itself which cause this male teacher so much pain in his personalizing the effects of "no touch" as he says, "*Recently, while on practicum a young boy came up to me and gave me a hug. I just froze, my mind was racing at a million miles an hour. Do I hug him back? If I do is that taking the student-teacher relationship too far? Why shouldn't I be able to give him a hug? Why should I be even having to think all this stuff?*"

I wouldn't have worked with children if I didn't feel connected with them emotionally, socially, and physically. Even though I now teach adults in the university setting I still feel similar (i.e., emotional, social, and physical) connections with my current students, feelings much like those I remember when working with young children. These feelings are not unlike those bell hooks (1994) describes when reexamining a relationship she had with one of her many university students. She describes the memorable class when a student:

> . . . came to class late and came right up to the front, picked me up and whirled me around. The class laughed. I called him 'fool' and laughed. It was by way of apologizing for being late, for missing any moment of the classroom passion. And so he brought his own moment. I, too, love to dance. And so we danced our way into the future as comrades and friends bound by all we had learned in class together. (pp. 197–198)

hooks (1994) notes that we must actively seek to "find again the place of eros within ourselves and together allow the mind and body to feel and know desire" (p. 199). Reflecting back to my earlier preschool teaching and thinking now of my current university teaching position, the discourse of desire helps me conceptualize and explain the ways I want to be with the children and adults whom I teach. When discussing different notions of desire in their book *Changing the Subject*, Henriques and colleagues (1984) state that "wishes and desires are based on needs that have once known satisfaction, to which, as it were, they hark back" (p. 213).

Other Stories of Desire: Teachers Who Touch

I solicited the following stories, from teachers and communities of caregivers which I knew to be advocates for touch. These respondents tended to make touch and issues of touch highly visible in their pedagogical practices (Garber 1995). Like those cases in the previous chapter, all of the teacher solicitations represented here responded to the "no touch" story broadcast on National Public Radio, "Day Care Center Goes to Extremes to Protect Reputation." They were asked several questions, including: (1) Do you touch children at your center? In what ways? (2) Are there any "no touch" policies where you work? (3) Do you think touch is important in early education?; and (4) What would you do if your director/principal informed you that you could not touch the children in your care?

In response to the first question, Do you touch children at your center? this group of teachers unanimously said *yes*, they touch children. The second part of the question asked, In what ways (do you touch)? A high school teacher answered, *"If they did a good job, I might pat them on the shoulder; when I worked with second graders last year I did hug them and put my arm around them."* A kindergarten "special needs" teacher said, "*I hug them and I pat them on the head, back, shoulders and arms. Since I work with special needs children I do a lot of hand-over-hand teaching to help them write, cut, and color. The kids I work with need a lot of encouragement, and sometimes words alone are not enough.*" After that, a preschool teacher shared, "*Touch is part of my job! For many reasons I feel the need and appropriateness of 'touching' (if a child misses his mom or dad and needs a hug, if a child falls down and gets hurt, or if a child simply wants a hug).*" The next teacher, a second grade teacher shared, "*My children often give me hugs at the end of the day, before leaving. Also, they use it to show appreciation when they enjoyed something we did in class. It is not uncommon for a child to run up to me in a hallway or in class and hug me or hold my hand.*" A third grade teacher said that, "*Everyday when the children leave for the day I stand at the door and give them a hug. Sometimes when they talk to me, I put my arm around them.*" Another teacher, who has been teaching sixth grade for four years said, "*I often will put my hand lightly on a child's back (like a pat) for praise. I sometimes lightly touch their hand or arm if I need them to focus. I shake hands with every student as they leave for the day. If students are receptive to hugs, I have no problem giving them a hug or an arm around their shoulder.*"

The next question asked was, Are there any "no touch" policies where you work? All teachers answered no. Then they responded to the question: Do you think touch is important in early education? The first teacher said, "*Yes. Touch is an essential element of our human-ness, it provides affirmation, it is nurturing. Children learn about their world through touch and are able to express love through touch.*" The next teacher shared, "*Yes, I believe touch is important in early education as well as upper grades. It can show appreciation, caring, attention that all children need to feel. It adds a personal side to what may sometimes be a seemingly impersonal environment to the child.*" The next teacher also said, "*Yes, because touch is a way to bond with the children and it helps them know that they are cared about.*" After those comments, another teacher said, "*Yes, it is important to calm children down when they are disturbed by something. Also, it makes my class feel good about being in school.*" The next teacher said "*Yes, children need to give free expression to their natural feelings. They need to feel wanted, cared for, loved and respected.*" Another teacher also said, "*Yes. It's* part of their emotional growth and development." Of the last two teachers, the first one said, "Yes, I do (when done 'appropriately' it shows that you care, or that you understand, or that you are proud of them, much more than words can do)." The final teacher responded, "Touch is one of the primary ways we, as humans, relate to one another. If we do not touch our children what message are we giving them?"

For the final question the teachers were asked, What would you do if your director/principal informed you that you could not touch the children in your care? In concert with the previous responses, the respondents shared: "It would be hard. I think my children would be sad and not as open with me. They would not be as enthusiastic, motivated or interested in learning." The next teacher said, "I would initially try to discuss the issue with him/her and I suppose if he/she stood firm, I guess I would have to abide by the rules (when they were around anyway!)." The next teacher shared, "I would try to explain to him/her why I think it is important and probably do it anyway." Another respondent shared, "I would try to do some research and surveys among other teachers and children on this policy and then report to a faculty meeting with the results." Another teacher said, "I would disagree with the policy. I would say that I have not seen any detrimental effects in my students. Yes, I would consider the implications, but I cannot see an absolute 'no touch' policy working, it's not in my personality either." The next teacher shared, "I can't believe there is such a thing as 'no touch' policy. I mean, I know there is but I think it is impossible to teach young children without touching them. If such a thing happened I'd see about getting a trained mediator come in and mediate, to talk with us and help us problem solve a 'happy medium' respecting administrative concerns and acknowledging the needs of young human beings. If not, I'd look to teach elsewhere." In similar fashion the next teacher said, "I could not continue to work in an environment that forbade touch in the classroom. I would educate the principal/director on the value and importance of touch. Fear seems to be the primary motive for the 'no touch' policy. Educating the administration would be the logical first step. Second, I would continue to give the children appropriate physical contact when needed. If my attempts to educate failed, they would need to fire me or I would voluntarily find another place of employment." The last teacher shared, "I would explain my rationale why I feel 'touching'

*is important, especially in early childhood education! I would ex-
plain and cite examples from my own experiences and any perti-
nent research."*

Commonalities

Like the stories shared in the previous chapter, these particular narratives represent only a small sample of teacher perspectives from a
particular source (e.g., teachers I knew to be advocates for touch), and
yet the commonalities these narratives share soon appear evident.
The dialogue from these stories runs in opposition to the "no touch"
stories presented earlier, as the teachers here discuss their willingness
to freely touch those children in their care, and to advocate for touch.
While reviewing the narrative commentary several common themes
appeared. These themes are further explored below, beginning with
the notions of the connection between theory and practice.

Connecting Theory and Practice

Many of the respondents discussed common classroom practices that
are complemented by their clear understandings of theories that support the importance of touch in human relationships. The type of
arguments they shared to bolster this understanding included comments like, *"Touch is an essential element of our human-ness, it
provides affirmation, it is nurturing"*; another commented, *"It can
show appreciation, caring, attention that all children need to feel"*;
another teacher commented that, *"Children need to give free expression to their natural feelings. They need to feel wanted, cared
for, loved and respected"*; another commented, *"It's part of their
emotional growth and development."* Lastly, a teacher shared, *"Touch
is one of the primary ways we relate to one another."*

These teachers have clearly thought through why touch is important to them and the children in their care. They back up what they do
in the classroom with supportive theoretical work that substantiates
not only their physical engagement with children, but their intellectual
engagement with touch. In a sense they have moved beyond their
traditional teacher education theoretical backgrounds as they are engaged in rethinking their practices. They have moved well beyond
allowing themselves to be "idealized" as traditional, historical representations. These teachers critically engage and attempt to move beyond what Yun Lee Too (1995) describes as the Socratic teacher ide-

als of the·"wise, non-materialist, moralist ascetic" (p. 9). Too argues that contemporary teachers, as pedagogues, are constantly under suspicion of failing to achieve this high ideal.

In the never-ending pursuit for achieving this now overly standardized, conservative ideal (Giroux 1996), McWilliam (1996) says that modern curricula and teachers themselves are made over as slick, "dismembered teachers, rendering them functionaries without self-interest, without desire, without any 'body' to teach (with)" (p. 313). Unlike the majority of teachers mentioned in chapter 4, because of their political ideals these advocates for touch don't engage in their pedagogical practices simply as "models to be imitated" (Too 1995, p. 186).

Political Awareness
Several of the respondents shared their willingness to politically engage the "no touch" debate and their unwillingness to back down from touching the children in their care. This is evidenced in their responses to the question, What would you do if your director/principal informed you that you could not touch the children in your care? Several of the respondents said they would conduct research/surveys to help educate other staff/parents about the importance of touch. Assuming what I think is a strong, radical stance, some of the teachers said, "*I'd look to teach elsewhere*" or "*I could not continue to work in an environment that forbade touch . . . if my attempts to educate them* [about the importance of touch] *failed, they would need to fire me or I would voluntarily find another place of employment.*"

I'm struck when considering the comment of the teacher who said she would, "*abide by the rules* [no touch] *when they were around,*" suggesting that she must then subvert the rules, go underground, and touch children only when the principal is not watching. This illustrates a great contradiction between touch as a typical aspect of everyday relationships with the children in her care, versus touch as some sort of subversive, revolutionary act which she can only engage in when it is safe.

Because they believe touch is an integral part of their duty of care and an integral part of all human relations, these teachers are willing to stand up for what they believe is important, to the point of putting their employment on the line. As the stories here illustrate, unlike those teachers who completely allow social control to define their subjectivity, many teachers are proactively working against "no touch"

policies that "manufacture . . . form, shape, and regulate, human desires" (Kelly 1997, p. 10) in ways they refuse to accept and are unwill-
ing to personally and professionally tolerate.

Touch Research Institute

Like the teachers above who believe in the importance of touch in
their professional lives, Tiffany Field is also a strong advocate for touch.
She is the founding Director of the Touch Research Institute (TRI), the
first center in the world devoted solely to the study of touch and its
application in science and medicine. Formally established in 1992 at
the University of Miami School of Medicine, TRI has conducted extensive interdisciplinary studies on the effects of massage therapy at all
stages of life, from newborns to senior citizens.

Research efforts that began in 1982 and continue today have shown
that touch, and more specifically touch therapy, has numerous benefi-
cial effects on human well being. The center currently supports sixty-
three different studies, ranging from premature infant to elderly adult
populations, all of which highlight the importance of touch. It is helpful here to share a small sample of the range of studies and the range
of topics that the TRI is pursuing, from newborn to elderly adult populations, includes:

(1) Full Term Infants of Depressed Mothers who were touched more experienced greater daily weight gain, more organized sleep/wake behaviors, less
fussiness, improved sociability and soothability, and improved interaction
behaviors;
(2) Cocaine Exposed Newborns provided with massage experienced increased
weight gain, better performance on the Brazelton Newborn Scale and reduced stress levels;
(3) Down's Syndrome Infants receiving massages at daycare are expected to
improve in muscle tone and in cognitive skills;
(4) Preschool children who received massage fell asleep sooner, exhibited
more restful nap time periods and had decreased activity levels;
(5) Cross Cultural Studies of Young Children's Touching—Studies are being
conducted on preschool playgrounds and at mealtimes in the home and at
McDonald's Restaurants in Paris and Miami to compare a high touch culture
(France) and low touch culture (United States);
(6) Preschool Touch—when data which showed that touch was rarely observed
in infant, toddler and preschool nurseries were presented to preschool teachers along with examples of appropriate touch, the amount of touch subse-
quently increased.

In addition, the Institute has conducted research on Cross Cultural Studies
on Adolescent Touch, Teenage Mothers' Childbirth Labor; Post Traumatic

Stress Disorder, Neglected and Abused Children, the effects of massage on Job Performance/Stress in adults, and the Effects of Grandparent Volunteers Providing Versus Receiving Massage. (Touch Research Institute 1997)

Closing

That the teachers and researchers whose stories are shared in this chapter are staunch advocates for the importance of touch in classrooms and in society, is an understatement. These teachers work proactively to make touch a critical part of their everyday pedagogical practices. Presented here as oppositional stories, the personal narratives these teachers share, "offer new ways of being political in the world" (Casey 1993, p. 157) of "no touch." They believe in the importance and power of touch for the formation and continuation of human relations. Dr. Tiffany Field and her associates at the Touch Research Institute continue to critically evaluate the wide-ranging effects of touch on human growth and development. The work of these teachers and researchers impacts children and society on a daily basis as they struggle, "systematically and patiently to form, develop, and render themselves and those with whom they work ever more homogeneous, compact and self-aware" (Gramsci 1980 p. 185, cited in Casey 1993, p. 162). Together they are working to make touch a vital part of the ongoing discourse on education and the care of infants, preschoolers, school-aged children, adolescents, adults, and senior citizens.

These caregivers are working against other growing discourses of "no touch," discourses that "record inappropriate desire and create spaces for it" (Stoler 1996, p. 177), like that of the National Educational Association's slogan, "Teach, don't touch" (Colt 1997). These professionals understand themselves to be in the full glare of public and institutional scrutiny, whether it be the medical school classroom or the elementary school teacher's lounge. By talking about touch and taking an active stance for touch, these teachers and researchers pursue a strong advocacy stance that seeks to work directly against what Purkiss (1994) describes as, "*not bringing it into a public sphere of debate and discussion, has the effect of privatising it, making it a space of no concern, an untheorised space of blankness on the map of professional identity*" (p. 193).

Chapter 5

The Sexual Dynamics of "Touching" Pedagogy

As sexual creatures, the need for understanding our sexual nature is always with us. Ignoring childhood sexuality does not make it go away.
—Sharon Heller, The Vital Touch

Don't touch yourself there, that's nasty.
—Kate Millet, Beyond Politics? Children and Sexuality

Perhaps we need to pay attention more to the absence of a current language in which people talk together or think about sexual realities rather than fictions. We need ways to visualize (beyond our own private agendas) the body and its foibles, its awkwardnesses, idiosyncrasies, fumblings and tentative possibilities. We need to address the silences around the real body—not that the 'real body' can be fully narrated, but there are certain absences and gaps in everyday discourse about the real body which now carry enormous consequences.
—Jill Lewis, "'So How Did Your Condom Use Go Last Night Daddy'"

Actively seeking space for a story to be told, I begin here by a story, my personal story of touch and desire—a story about me and my infant daughter. It goes like this:

The sensation of the palm of my hand gently caressing her bare back pleases me and by the contented, rhythmic sound of her breathing she seems equally encouraged with this interaction. With her arms gently placed around me we sit together, mostly silent with the exception of an occasional whisper while I continue running my hands and fingers over her skin. It is with great intent that my hand searches out each possible spot on this bare part of her body. At times she stops me by taking my hand and removing it and at other times she redirects my touch, again taking my hand, but this time guiding it to another part of her body where she prefers to be touched. Sometimes my hands and fingers roam quickly

over her body and other times they pause long enough to briefly massage
a part of her skin. Typically this gratifying interaction is initiated and led
by me and tends to stop only when my desires have been fulfilled, but I
won't speak for her, I can't speak for her. (Johnson 1997d).

This story describes a daily interaction(s) for me, most of which takes place well after my daughter Haleigh is fast asleep in my arms at the end of a long stay in a rocking chair, just before she is placed in her bed for what I'm hoping will be a long rest. I wrote this personal narrative recognizing that we have to actively seek out space(s) for a voice to be found, for a sexual story to be told (Plummer 1995). If we wish to collectively fight against "no touch" policies, then we must be willing to intellectualize our understandings of sexualities (Eisen and Hall 1996) as we seek to better understand ourselves and the children we care for (Johnson 1997e; Richter 1997).

This chapter explores sexuality as a way of reconceptualizing how we theorize the effects of "no touch" in early childhood and primary education. To this end, the attempt here is to rethink "no touch," moving away from the traditional humanist perspective(s) that framed much of chapter 1. To further ground this critique I illustrate how sexuality is positioned within the grand early childhood narrative(s), so well represented in many of the "no touch" stories presented earlier and within popular early childhood texts. Ultimately this section critiques popular notions of sexuality in early childhood education.

While the notion of *moral panic* has been helpful in my initial interrogations of much of the hysteria surrounding "no touch" (see Johnson 1995, 1997c, and 1997d), another area that I now see warrants attention in this project is the study of sexuality. Over the past several years broad sexuality concerns have been very much in the forefront of state and national politics in America, Australia, and other parts of the world (Altman 1995; Fout 1992; Grosz and Probyn 1994; Segal 1994). Current exemplar issues, several of which were mentioned earlier, include the publishing of the *Paedophilia Index* in New South Wales, Australia; banning of same sex marriages; federal funding of allegedly obscene art; the sexual content of public school curricula—like the Anne Arundel County school system which recently removed Maya Angelou's *I Know Why the Caged Bird Sings* from the ninth-grade curriculum, a book that describes the author's childhood and includes descriptions of rape, abuse, and sexual anxiety about lesbianism; removing federal dollars from school districts that use curriculum materials that teach about homosexuality; the content of safe-sex education; and the popular elementary education publication, *Weekly Reader* and *Time for Kids*, which teachers throughout America use to teach broad curricular content, refuse to print stories that discuss sexuality and President Clinton's impeachment hearings (Duggan, 1995).

More specific sexuality issues that have recently marked the field of early childhood education include the extent of sexual abuse of children in day-care centers; implementing center-based policies that disallow men from changing diapers; widespread fingerprinting and criminal checks of day-care workers; incorporating "good touch" and "bad touch" practices into early schooling curricula; and a society-wide willingness to portray all males who (desire to) teach young children as perverts (Johnson 1997; Pally 1994; Silin 1997).

Like gender, sexuality provides one of the "basic narratives through which our identities are forged. We become aware of our individual identity first and foremost, as a gendered one, and gender differences themselves draw upon what are seen as fundamental differences between male and female sexuality" (Segal 1997, p. xii). Today we can't think of such issues as "power, the family, the organization of work, identity and politics" without a clearer understanding of sexuality. Weeks and Holland (1996) note that "Sexuality is shaped within society, and in turn helps to make and remake the variety of social relations . . . a sociology which ignores the sexual will fail to grasp the complexity of identities, belongings, personal relationships and social meanings in late modern societies" (p. 13). Sexuality is a vital, necessary aspect of human experience, and remains a pressing social issue throughout our society(ies) (Casper et alia 1996; Corbett 1991; Klein 1992; Lewis 1997; Valverde 1987).

Popular Notions of Sexuality: What the Texts Teach Us about Touch?

To gain an understanding of the different ways that sexuality is viewed in early childhood education, I studied popular discourses of this topic (in this case, textual evidence) in the field of early childhood education. To assist in this process I reviewed content on *sexuality* from a wide variety of popular early education texts, those books that would grace the early childhood library collections in teacher education programs throughout the world. I chose these particular texts because many of them were used when I was an early childhood master's and doctoral student, some of them I've used before in early childhood education "Foundations" courses, they were all available in several university libraries in the United States and Australia, and the majority of them have been reprinted multiple times. These texts clearly have holding power as knowledge sources in early childhood education.

In order to conduct the text analysis I looked up the word "sexuality" in the index of each text that was reviewed. When that word/descriptor wasn't available I then looked up related terms, including sex, sex-role development, gender, social development, etc. A brief review of my preliminary findings begins with a chapter entitled, "Science Activities" in the book, *Introduction to Early Childhood Education* (Hildebrand 1986b). In this particular passage the author shares,

> Another important aspect of the child's self-concept is sex role identification. Most children are happy with their own sex, and the teacher should help a child to play and understand the concept of maleness and femaleness . . . boys and girls under 6 typically share the same bathroom at school. Such an arrangement provides a healthy environment for learning valuable sex information. Children will look at each other's bodies during the toileting. They will also ask questions that can be answered factually. (p. 230)

Later in this section the discussion on sex finishes with the following words of wisdom:

> The handling of genitals, or masturbation, is generally a harmless activity and is often observed in young children. Masturbation may have various meanings, so a child must be observed individually so that the purpose of masturbation for a given child can be discovered. Of course, masturbation can mean the child is insecure and unhappy. However, it can also mean the child is bored and needs active play, or that clothing is too tight . . . teachers must have an enlightened attitude around shaming the child. (p. 231)

Joanne Hendrick's book, *The Whole Child: Developmental Education for the Early Years* (1996) informs us:

> Today, when educational emphasis tends to be placed on the value of nonsexist education, it may be necessary to remind the reader that it is also important to teach children about reproduction and gender difference and to help them value their maleness or femaleness. (p. 353)

In one of Hendrick's other books, *Total Learning: Developmental Curriculum for the Young Child* (1997), the reader is reminded, "Many adults feel uneasy about discussing sex and reproduction with children. Fortunately for those of us who feel awkward about this subject, the questions nursery school-age children ask are likely to be simple and not very distressing" (p. 193). Later in that same section the reader is reminded, "In discussions about reproduction, teachers should find out what the children really want to know, make answers truthful and simple, encourage children to say what they think . . ." (p. 194).

In another text, *Foundations of Early Childhood Education: Teaching Three, Four, and Five-Year-Old Children,* the authors share, "Increasingly early childhood educators have been expected to deal with a wide range of social problems including child sexual abuse and neglect, substance abuse (drugs or alcohol), and sex education" (Spodek, Saracho, and Davis 1991, p. 68). Other than this passage, nowhere else in this "Foundational" text is sexuality or sex discussed.

In the book, *Behaviors of Preschoolers and Their Teachers* (Carson and Sykes 1991), the authors share a multitude of narrative accounts they observed and recorded when crafting an ethnography of life in preschool classrooms. After each anecdotal account is presented the authors then debrief the passage. One particular narrative flows in the following manner:

> By this time of day I am ready to lie down on the cots with the children. Worked with Mark today, the child is strange like his father. Oh did he put on a show for his teachers today! I do know that he humps the cot as if it were some long lost female companion. My best advice to the teachers is to ignore his behavior unless it commences to disrupt the other children . . . or involves them. After all, what does a four-year-old know except a bunch of sensation guided by an erratic mental compass? (Carson and Sykes 1991, p. 162)

After this all-too-brief deconstruction of the observation the authors then advise the reader to, "Ignore behaviors that are only minimally disruptive and that are of no harm to others. A teacher cannot expect to respond to every behavior of each and every child, so save your energy and attention for the more significant behaviors" (p. 163). Later in the text, when discussing issues of what to say when asked about boy-girl stuff, the authors offer, "Just listen to them when preschoolers ask about boy-girl stuff. Adults often make the mistake of proffering up, usually with a red face, more complexity or depth than the child needs, wants, or can intellectually accommodate" (p. 184).

In her text, *The Whole Child: Developmental Education for the Early Years* (1996) Hendrick states: "The more open and matter-of-fact teachers and parents can be about differences in the anatomy of boys and girls, the more likely it is that children will not need to resort to 'doctor' play or hiding in corners to investigate such differences" (p. 354).

Etaugh and Rathus (1995) explain that their comprehensive early education text, *The World of Children*, ". . . communicates in content and form the excitement, relevance, and true scientific nature of the discipline of child development" (p. vii). Five hundred and eighty-six pages later, just before the end of this text, the authors get at the "excitement, relevance, and true scientific nature" of sexuality, embedded in a chapter on "Adolescence."

Even early childhood texts that devote themselves solely to sexuality don't necessarily push the issues much beyond the normative discourse patterns presented above. For example, in the text, *Sexual Development of Young Children* (Lively and Lively 1991) the authors say that while talking to children about sexuality,

> It is appropriate to answer a child's questions at the time it is asked, but it is unwise to answer with details beyond the child's level of understanding. It is important to be frank but strictly to the point and limited to the topic of the moment. Children are sexual beings as are all of us . . . In essence the teacher's role is to allow any discussion of sexual matters that fits into the educational process . . . Teachers should be as helpful in areas of sexuality as in specialized topics such as art and music. (p. 43)

Later in their book, in their further critique of sexuality and gender, the Lively's go so far as to make sexists comments:

> *Evidence does not support the view that a strong mother and a weak father is likely to cause the male child to be homosexual. On the other hand, allowing a boy to behave in a feminine manner and dress in girl's clothing without being discouraged may have some impact. These behaviors, combined with a rejection of rough and tumble play, may cause an isolation from the male environment.* (p. 4)

To help further frame this critique it is important to note how sexuality is positioned within the grand early childhood narrative(s), so well represented in the various texts reviewed here. The topic "Sexuality" was never a stand-alone chapter in any of the texts I reviewed. Depending on the text, sexuality as a topic shares textual space in chapters that discuss "Multiculturalism," "Sexual Abuse," "Social Science," "Special Relationships," and "Providing Cross-Cultural, Non-sexist Education." One text included sexuality issues within the "Science Activities" chapter. Further, the major headings or subheadings that help frame sexuality as important early childhood education knowledge/course content, included the following titles:

1. Teaching Simple Physiological Facts
2. Masturbation
3. Meeting the Special Needs of Boys in the Preschool
4. Sex Role Identification
5. Gender Role Development

The sexuality content I did find in these texts was dominated by traditional notions which treat sexuality as simple, unifying, conservative themes (Foucault 1984b; McNay 1991). As taught in these texts, as taught in our classes, sexuality in early childhood education is all about the normative practices of reproduction (i.e., penis and vagina), social studies (one of the texts informs us, "Thinking of it as a 'geography' question can make it reasonably unembarrasing to explain that a baby is growing inside the mother's uterus or that it will be born through a special hole women have between their legs . . .") and science (e.g., another text tells us, "Some children handle their genitals more than others. This is called masturbation. It gives children a pleasurable sensation and is sometimes comforting").

In their recent book, *Rethinking Sex: Social Theory and Sexuality Research*, Connell and Dowsett suggest that, "Sexuality is a major theme in our culture, from the surf video to the opera stage to the papal encyclical. It is accordingly, one of the major themes of the human sciences" (1992, p. 49). Yet, in my cursory review of these early childhood textbooks, I had to search rather hard to find sexuality in the topical index. Most of the texts reviewed here steer well clear of using the word at all. In many of these popular early childhood books, you are more likely to find "Toilet Training" in the index than you are "Sexuality." These baseline data reveal that in colleges/schools of education, and in the larger field of early childhood education in general, the popular discourse around childhood sexuality is a discourse focused not on teaching about sexuality, but on teaching *around* sexuality—a process of erasure.

Reframing Sexuality in Early Childhood Education

Ken Plummer recently noted that, "Anyone who writes about sex these days stands at the intersection of a vast literature speaking about sex

from every conceivable persuasion" (1995, p. x). Yet, the scant literature and research in the field of early childhood education seem to be
quite distant from the "intersection" Plummer notes. Even while critical issues of sexuality continue to present themselves in one form or
another to our field (Dollimore 1991; Gagnon and Parker 1995; Grosz
and Probyn 1994; Haste 1994; Irvine 1995), other oppositional move-
ments intent on "renaturalizing and reinstating 'ideal' or 'necessary'
forms of relations" with children and families (Johnson 1996) gain
more notice and, instead, are placed at the forefront. At the same time
that a wide variety of issues of sexuality should have dominated the
popular discourses in early education (Kenway 1996), what we've instead focused on is our typical, traditional return to safety and normalcy (Grosz 1995; Walkerdine 1984).

These normative discourses are readily evidenced in a recent issue
of the popular early childhood journal *Young Children*. This widely
read journal is included as part of membership benefits for all those
who join the National Association for the Education of Young Children (NAEYC). It is a quarterly journal that reaches well over 100,000
members, the largest mass of early educators worldwide. The September 1997 issue included a story called, "Becoming sexual: Differences between child and adult sexuality" (Rothbaum, Grauer, and Rubin
1997). In attempting to set the reader/practitioner in the field of early
education at ease, these authors critique childhood sexuality by com-
paring it to adult sexuality.

The authors ground this critique by noting that children and adults
differ in three specific areas of sexuality: curiosity and play, spontane-
ity and openness, and sensuality and excitement. Like the majority of
the major theoretical underpinnings in early education, this article
approaches sexuality in a strict, fundamentally developmentalist manner. Several citations witness this fact, including, ". . . critical aspects
of human functioning develop in stages from infancy through adult-
hood" (p. 22); "[children's use of] Terms such as poo poo, pee pee,
fart, penis . . . butt-face and penis breath . . . is eminently normal
behavior" (p. 24); ". . . most demonstrations of physical affection
initiated by children-hugging, kissing, and other sensual touching or
stroking, owe more to attachment needs than to Eros" (p. 25);
"Children's play involving sexual roles and relationships is universal"
(p. 25); and "Young children are innocent in that they are curious,
playful, open, spontaneous, sensual, and excited" (p. 28).

While attempting to address an area of seemingly vital concern
(i.e., "intersection of a vast literature" that Plummer notes) in early

education, this article instead fails to take a critical stance. One could argue that the fact that a potentially controversial issue like sexuality is presented in a professional journal supported by only ten dated research article citations (which date from 1948 through 1991), reveals the uncritical nature of this particular narrative. Once again, normalcy and safety are the thematic issues strictly adhered to throughout this narrative, throughout the field of early education. The field of early education at-large continues valorizing conservative, singular, humanist perspectives on children and their sexual/developmental progression (i.e., child development as staged-based, "universal" phenomena; "normal behavior"; "child as innocent"; "attachment not Eros") while other more radical perspectives remain mostly silenced.

And so our "talk" about sex in early education "enables certain normative discourse (e.g., Foucault's 'medicine of sex') to emerge and be sustained" (Haywood 1996; Madus 1995; Wagener 1998). Again, these views run counter to the notion that sexuality takes on "many forms, patterned in a variety of different ways . . . and cannot be understood outside the context in which it is enacted, conceptualized and reacted to" (Weeks and Holland 1996, p. 1).

We've all witnessed this "talk" enacted all the time in our early childhood education courses, in our respective academic settings. For example, during a typical debriefing period about field experiences, practicum students share with the larger class a "real life" story they encountered out in the field. This is a story of sexuality, again, a highly typical story we all face each semester. It goes something like this:

Professor: "Who would like to share a story from your practicum?"

Student: "Today at my prac I noticed one of the three-year-old boys standing by himself behind a tree for a very long time. After a while I began to wonder what he was doing over there by himself so I wandered over to check it out. When I looked behind the tree I discovered the front of his pants were drawn down and he was playing with his, his . . . penis. It was erect and he told me, 'It won't go down!' I didn't know what to say, what to do, so I went to the lead teacher and informed her about this incident."

Professor: "What did you say to the boy?"

Student: "Well, nothing, I didn't know what to say!"

Professor: "Well as you all know from your reading, this kind of thing is normal for that age child, especially for boys. It is called masturbation. All children do it, even girls, and it typically happens around age three to four. It is part of normal, healthy child development so don't worry about it and don't embarrass the child. If you haven't observed it yet you will sometime during your practicum experiences or while you have your own classroom. OK, now let's move on and talk about whole language!"

I remember this type of interaction all too well when I was both an undergraduate and graduate student in early childhood education. Our education didn't follow from our needs and wants and focus on what hooks (1994) advocates, "Realizing that my students were uncertain about expressions of care and love in the classroom, I found it necessary to teach on the subject" (p. 198). Instead of recognizing our needs issues of sexuality were never questioned ("*It is part of normal, healthy child development so don't worry about it and don't embarrass the child*") and were always presented as unproblematic, "fundamental, invariable truths about the nature of children." These traditional, dominant discourses of the field are "as true for the children of today as for the children of a century ago; for the children of Newcastle as the children of New York or New Delhi" (Stainton Rogers and Stainton Rogers 1992, p. 51). The body of research on children and sexuality closely matches the inscripted *body* (Grosz 1994; 1995) of the young child—a pure, innocent, fragile, and immature *body* indeed. We capitalize on these notions of children, as Millet notes (1984), ". . . adults have been all too effective, not only in poisoning sexuality but also in preventing children from understanding or experiencing it" (p. 218).

Even while we pretend sexuality is not an important issue, that it doesn't exist for children and for the field of early childhood education, our ignorance protects us and keeps us theoretically safe. We remain ignorant and silent at a time when we know children of all ages understand sexual life (Johnson 1996; Lees 1993). Our fearfulness and suspicion keep us at a safe distance from sexuality (Irvine 1995). We do this at a time when sexuality has shifted from the margins to the center in many disciplines highly familiar and interrelated to our own work (Adkins and Merchant 1996). We model our early childhood practices as we model our sexuality interactions with children by assuming, "We have a need for children to be ignorant. In the face of evidence that they know a lot about sex and birth and even about AIDS and death, we continue to insist that they don't know, can't know, shouldn't know" (Tobin 1997, p. 136). Certainly this ignorance and silence carries well over into adult sexuality issues during this era of AIDS awareness. As an example, the Moral Right agenda has more successfully used sexuality issues to promote the protection of the "patriarchal, nuclear family" (Lewis 1997). While this campaign is pretending to be busily "protecting the family," they/we have in fact failed to protect real lives, as safe sex practices have witnessed only moderate success (i.e., condom users are still in the minority), adolescents continue to become sexually active at earlier ages and sexually transmitted diseases are at epidemic proportions (Center on the Family 1995; Durham 1997).

It seems this need for children to be ignorant and innocent carries well over into our practices as the text review here illustrates we have a similar, profound need for academics, teachers, and caregivers (i.e., our collective selves) to be ignorant in their/our understandings of sexuality. Duggan (1995) notes that our "muteness is expected . . . enforced by the logic of a sex panic . . . if you are accused of sexual 'deviance,' your defensive strategies are limited to either confession and repentance, or denials of personal 'guilt', both of which only reinforce the legitimacy" (p. 75). At the same time our ignorance and our self-muted voices actively protect us, they are actively harming others. At a time when we should be enlarging the spaces for intellectual deliberations about sexuality to be heard, we have instead reduced the dialogue on sexuality. The danger in this is noted by Vance (1984) as she states, "When pleasure occupies a smaller and smaller public space and a more guilty private space, individuals do not become empowered; they are merely cut off from the source of their own strength and energy" (p. 7).

As a member of the field of early childhood education I feel that I/ we, have indeed "ignored the sexual, failed to grasp the complexity of identities" (Bristow 1997; Tiefer 1995). The "cultural scripts" (McCormick 1994) of my profession enable me to know little about sexuality and young children. I well know, firsthand, how much we've ignored the sexual—I recognized it as a teacher of young children; I recognized it as a graduate student studying at several prestigious early childhood education programs; I recognized it as an academic working in established early childhood programs in different parts of the United States and beyond; and I recognize it now after studying it here.

Given the strong movement toward "no touch" policy in early education, we cannot continue to justify our efforts to physically interact with children, to touch, or take a stance against "no touch" without engaging issues of identity, desire, intimacy, and sensuality in critical, intellectual ways. Our now common exclusionary "no touch" pedagogical practices (Sibley 1995), and our inability to critically interrogate and stand up to "no touch" policy has influenced the field in negative ways. When we can honestly recognize and critically confront our own diverse sexual identities and those of the children in our care, then maybe we can begin to move forward in our further understandings of sexuality.

Chapter 6

Soothing a Crying Child in the Age of "No Touch"

*This function of moral and political storytelling is sometimes referred to
as communal truth-telling, in which the play of call and response gener-
ates a shared understanding of the way things are.*
—Audrey Thompson, *Not the Color Purple: Black Feminist Lessons for
Educational Caring*

*Caregivers have the power to comfort or not. In not comforting, they
exert negative power, as opposed to the healing, nurturing, transformative
power . . .*
—Robyn Leavitt, *Power and Emotion in Infant-Toddler Daycare*

A central question, one that repeatedly emerges from the many discussions with groups of practitioners and parents I've met with over
the past five years is, What does it (i.e., adult-child, adult-adult, child-
child interactions) look like in a "no touch" environment? Whenever
this question arises, a question I've been personally asking myself
from the very beginning of my engagement with this issue, I've tried
in my head to visualize "no touch" practices. Visualizing in my head
and transferring that visualization, that picture, onto these pages has
been an important part of this project (Heller 1996). Through this
writing I've tried to make "no touch" clear in my head, so clear that
my eyes not only see, they listen, as this "writing becomes audible,
legible, intelligible" (Zavala 1992, p. 145) for me and for others. If I
accomplish this task then many others can visualize "no touch" themselves, whether or not they share the same caregiver experiences with
me, whether or not they work in caregiving professions, whether they
have young children or not.

The visualization of "no touch" practices in my head is deeply influenced by many factors. One part of me, the infant/toddler caregiver

and preschool teacher of twenty years ago, retrospectively sees my-self changing the diapers of the infant boys and girls in my care, rock-ing newborns to sleep, hugging children to greet, console, and wish them farewell, and exchanging other forms of touch. One part of me, the "me" now deeply entrenched in today's world of "no touch," visu-alizes a young, tall male teacher standing in front of a crying first grade child. I can visualize this teacher with his arms crossed, folded firmly against his chest. He looks down at the crying child and asks her "What happened, are you OK?" Even as he finds out more infor-mation, as the child's cry slowly softens into a whimper, his arms remain folded. Another part of me visualizes myself, a father of three young children, totally disregarding "no touch" while realizing that touch is a critical aspect of many, if not most, of my interactions with my children, just as it was with the children I cared for as a teacher/ caregiver. As a father and as a teacher of young children, the cases that I'm most familiar with and emotionally attached to, are continu-ing to encounter oppositional discourses, oppositional narratives like the vignette of the male teacher presented above. As I try to recall my cherished memories of touch, what I once easily visualized, what was once so clear, has now become hazy. "No touch," which once seemed quite distant and foreign has become too familiar.

Visualizing Touch

Much of my personalizing throughout this book has been dominated by self-reflection, remembering a time when I taught young children on a daily basis. Enacting this reflective, self-inquiry practice once more, I remember when I first worked with two-year-old children. My mentor teachers taught me to greet children at the door so that I could physically and emotionally assist with the all-important transition time as parents (typically the mother back then) separated from children. In most cases this separation was for the first time in this still novel parent-child relationship. Among other feelings, this separation typi-cally brought child and adult tears, child cries and a physical pulling (sometimes prying) away as the caregiver left the child in our care and each began the long day apart from one another.

As a practicum student learning how to teach young children, my main job was to help children relax, providing warm, supportive physical assistance while children physically and emotionally separated from their caregivers. The primary mode of this emotional and physical assistance involved touch. Whether it involved holding a child back from running out to an exiting mother or carrying a child to a rocking chair, or stroking a child's back while rocking them during a soothing transition time, touch was an instrumental part of this caregiving experience. It began first thing in the morning and continued throughout the day. Again, these memories of touch are remarkably present in my existence now and the memory brings a smile to my face and a sense of calm to my inner being as a teacher. These memories define my subjectivity as a caregiver/teacher as much in the present as they did in the past.

When I now compare these memories to the current caregiver/teacher narratives I'm taken aback. I can't visualize the same separations I experienced in today's "no touch" environment(s). I can't visualize a nap time that doesn't include rubbing a child's back while helping them to fall off to sleep. I can't visualize working in a classroom that doesn't allow me change diapers. What I can visualize are classrooms today where children never experience the selfless, nurturant caregiver who would go to all extremes possible to calm the hungry, screaming six-week-old, soothe the tired toddler, and make the stressful morning separation as tolerable as possible for the anxious three- or four-year-old. In the "no touch" classrooms of today children and caregivers surely are less likely to experience the sensuality of touch, witness the free exchange of physical contact, and have the freedom to enact what they are learning about the theoretical importance of touch during their many typical interactions with each other.

Visualizing "No Touch"

As was mentioned earlier in chapter 3, caregivers and teachers alike have little problem remaining visible, under surveillance, and under the watchful "no touch" gaze of numerous others during their time working with children. After all we now "live in a 'society of the spectacle,' in which the saturation of images distracts us from the connections that form communities" (Heller 1996, p. A8). As an example, witness this "saturation" in the follow story, as a veteran teacher informs a practicum student:

> The rule is, don't touch kids, but in kindergarten a hug is sometimes what they need. By law it is safe not to touch a child at all, so you never have to face child abuse charges. Sexual abuse cases are many in the schools so if you don't touch, you won't have that problem too. The teacher's union representative will say never, never touch a child!!!!

The spectacle has become so powerful that our collective community memories of how we could/should be interacting with (i.e., touching) children, memories like mine that were once crystal clear in our collective minds, have now become clouded, obscured by reactionary guilt, paranoia, litigation, over-protection, and surveillance. As many of the stories shared throughout this book illustrate, we have now created a new consciousness, new memories, about how we should interact with children in our care. Those who work with children today share recent memories that are more replete with practices they shouldn't follow while caring for children (e.g., keep your hands to yourself; leave the doors and windows open; don't be alone with children; don't let males change diapers; and don't allow children to sit on your lap), than practices they should follow. The recent memories which now seem to be so deeply ingrained in our collective conscience, tend to be more focused on protecting our adult selves than on serving (i.e., protecting) children.

How Children Visualize the
Disengagement of Adult Caregivers

Even though all of the stories collected, presented, and critiqued here are in some way about children, these stories do not directly reflect children's voices. While this particular project is more about how what adults do impacts adults and children, I think it is critical here to single out children and consider "no touch" as it influences them and their everyday experiences with adults and with each other. I'm interested here in what children are doing with "no touch," what they are making of it, and what potentially happens to them in the midst of all this. Amidst all of the theoretical debates and adult practitioner "stories from the field" the active, embodied, passionate lives of children, the group of beings ultimately most effected by "no touch," remain silenced. While "no touch" stories have dominated the discussion up until now, I think it is more appropriate to speak of touch by envisioning narratives of touch, as those stories relate to children.

This current project does not include children voices and I don't want to necessarily speak for children or suggest that I ever could. What I do want to do is bring to bear my more than twenty years of experience working with and caring for children from settings as diverse as hospital playrooms, pediatric wards, after-school care environments, infant-toddler and preschool classrooms, supervising undergraduate teacher education students placed in elementary class-rooms, coaching children's sports, and my eleven years of parenting experience. I've witnessed and participated in the birth of my three children and the death of other children in pediatric oncology wards. I've been around children and I've witnessed a lot over the years. It is the labor of these experiences from which I will speak here.

From the very moment of birth when the infant is, for the first time, outside of the mother's womb and yet still connected through warm hugs to the mother's (and sometimes father's) body, touch is critical to the growth and development of this newborn. As studies of touch-deprived children reveal touch remains important throughout child-hood. Returning once more to Tiffany Field's research at the Touch Research Institute (TRI), we see how field studies validate the impor-tance of touch. Researchers at TRI have studied the effects of massage on cocaine, addicted newborns, colicky infants, sexually abused infants, and those with depressed mothers, as well as children with asthma, skin disorders, diabetes, burns, cystic fibrosis, and juvenile rheuma-toid arthritis. Field's research illustrates that

> Massaged babies often show greater weight gain, fewer postnatal complica-tions, and decreased cortisol levels. They are more social, more alert, less fussy and restless, sleep better, and have smoother movement . . . After one month of fifteen-minute touch therapy sessions twice a week, preschool au-tistic children, who suffer from extreme touch aversion, were more willing to be touched, and showed less autistic behavior. (Heller 1997, p. 38)

Studies like those conducted at TRI and other current and historical works are quickly discounted when we move the child(ren) from one institution, the hospital, and relocate them to another institution, the classroom. We have the same people, placed in very similar institu-tions (i.e., places which are supposed to help people), yet we follow very different rules of care. If rules of care, or the duty of care are about caring for children, the institution alone should not dictate how that care is conducted. The caregiving relationship should predicate my duty of care, and, if the duty of care calls for me to provide, "An enduring bond [which] is sustained through an authentic relation-ship" (Slunt 1994), the authenticity I bring to that duty includes touch as a critical part of the way I nurture and care for children.

Even though much of the historical and recent research on touch was conducted in more controlled, artificial contexts (orphanages and hospitals), when I worked with children in other institutions (child-care centers and school classrooms), I immediately witnessed how the theory generalized to my caregiving practices. I saw how my soothing touch(es) calmed the colicky infant, how my physical and social behavior in the rocking chair soothed the overly tired newborn, how the tip of my pinky finger inserted into the crying newborns mouth simulated mother's nipple acting like a pacifier and calmed baby, and how my lap acted as a safe space for the two-year-old needing assistance after a scuffle with a peer. From my everyday experiences with children it was easy to see the crossover from theory to practice, from the textbook to real life. Children clearly witnessed and experienced that touch mattered in their care. I clearly witnessed that touch mattered in the care of children.

Not only did I see it, I liked how it felt to provide that care. I liked being the caregiver who calmed the screaming infant, or the teacher who used touch to calm the temper tantrum kicking, out-of-control three-year-old. Based on my anecdotal observations, children have always seemed to like that teacher/caregiver side of me that touch(es), as I physically helped to calm and settle their erratic behaviors, and they positively responded to how I expressed my subjectivity as a nurturant adult. Too, they witnessed that touch was an important part of my duty of care. It was and still is what I am about as a caregiver. All of the children I've worked with learned to expect this and trust that this duty of care would be an integral part of my daily interactions, my daily engagements, with them. In the present world of "no touch" I don't think that similar expectations of the duty of care, this same sense of trust, can occur now if we allow "no touch" practices to govern who we are as caregivers and teachers. I don't think I could've been as engaged as I was as a caregiver/teacher if I taught in a world dominated by "no touch" discourses.

I understand that duty of care can and should include many different understandings, but as I discuss it above and as Slunt (1994) explained it earlier, a primary aspect of it involves engagement with the children in my care. As a caregiver, this engagement with the children in my care manifests itself socially, emotionally, intellectually, and physically. Just as I socially and emotionally try to be responsive to children without holding back, I do the same by physically and intellectually engaging them. Critiquing "no touch" from this integrative perspective, I could interrogate the absurdity of "no touch" as being about as practical as "no laugh," "no cry," or "no talk" classroom practices might be. What would those practices look like? Can we have any one without the other(s)? Can I single out and not participate in certain physically responsive aspects of my duty of care and still call myself a good teacher? Is this of ethical importance to me, to parents, to our respective professions?

If I chose not to participate in emotional aspects of my duty of care I believe I would be jeopardizing the healthy growth and development of the children in my charge. The same would be true of social or intellectual considerations. Yet, even though "no touch" automatically implies we are not being physically responsive to the toddlers or first graders we care for, we fail to question that aspect. The teachers and caregivers, administrators and parents who readily accept the tenets of "no touch" are labeling themselves as physically unresponsive to children and their needs. Just as we collectively embody this unresponsive attitude we are "ignoring, suppressing, denying, and leaving unclarified" (Leavitt 1994, p. 58) children's emotional beings. Although the inherent danger of the physically unresponsive "no touch" practices remains quite obvious, a more pressing concern may be that the children involved in these adult practices (e.g., withholding of affection, refusal to comfort, physical rejection) are being emotionally abandoned (Leavitt 1994), beginning at a very young age. Again, as they comply with "no touch" policies, teachers today who are more concerned with teaching practices they "should not" follow, are being told by society (and are telling themselves) to emotionally abandon the very persons they are supposed to be caring for. Is this what we want? Is this what children want, and deserve?

Imagining Responsive Care—Is Soothing Children Enough?

Imagine responsive care. Picture in your mind what responsive care looks like. Imagine responsive care. The absurdity of "no touch" is I now have to imagine in my mind, what touching, responsive caregiving looks like, because from what the "no touch" narratives here tell me, I have to search hard to actually see this kind of caregiving in real life. In the past few years I've had to think harder and harder about what the "good old days" were like, days when we still allowed touching, when I touched the children in my care all the time. Caregiver and teachers who desire engaging, responsive relationships are somehow now estranged practitioners. Those who are willing to engage, to transgress these safe, newly defined self-imposed duties of care, put themselves at great risk by even considering allowing a child to sit on their lap, let alone hug a child, hence the previous chapter heading "Strange Stories of Desire." Given the way and the rate which things have progressed I don't have to consider males in any of these equations. I can't, for they have been erased out of the equation(s). Male caregivers who can't change diapers, who have been placed in the upper grades for their own protection, who ask their female colleagues to check the bathrooms for any stray children. In our hasty abdication from common sense caregiver practices that were once not only expected, but demanded, we've thrown out a vital principle of good practices, and are, instead, reverting to police-state surveillance tactics, all for the supposed good of the children, for their safety and protection!

This chapter begins with the title "Soothing a Crying Child in the Age of 'No Touch'," but clearly "no touch" issues reach well beyond the simple caregiving processes of soothing. While my chief concerns about the effects of "no touch" lie mostly with children, I am also very concerned about caregivers, parents, and ultimately society. In my continued discussions with caregivers, teachers, and parents, I witness that we've lost a lot of ground even in the past several years when I began studying these phenomena. The stories that I thought were incredibly absurd four years ago pale in comparison to the stories I continue to hear today. Last month a caregiver informed me that while her center has no formal "no touch" policies, caregivers must raise their voices and speak loudly while changing diapers because the diaper changing areas lie behind a wall, placing them behind easy sight lines of colleagues and parents. The loud voice, a witness to all others on the opposite side of the diaper changing wall, replaces the protective eyes and allows the child and caregiver to remain under constant surveillance. In that same discussion another caregiver said that at her center teachers were told by the director that they are not allowed to touch children on the chest (read breast). Indeed, we have lost a lot of ground!

Even though I've had to think harder to get clear on the issues here, I can't give in to "no touch" and simply allow it to enter early childhood discourses uncontested. That would be too easy. Like each of my colleagues in all of the field settings I work, we must continue to challenge ourselves and each other

> to examine ways in which we can transcend our circumstances to imagine different futures . . . by talking about the assumptions underlying our work, by creating an inclusive space in which we invite others to the table, by

problematizing our own privilege . . . by making local change in our thera-
peutic and research practices, we can make change. (O'Loughlin 1997,
p. 21)

We need to collectively work against "no touch" by recognizing,
clearly stating, and being proud of what it means to be a caregiver/
teacher of young children. Beginning with the recognition that this is
a critical issue in our professional and personal lives will help caregivers
become more self-aware of the impact of "no touch" on their practices and how that affects the children they care for. Our activist work
can create new boundaries, offer new possibilities for touch/"no touch"
discourses (Delandshere and Petrosky 1994). Leavitt's (1994) work
helps me understand the importance of this self-inquiry. Like the activist stance that O'Loughlin takes, Leavitt feels that as caregivers we
must "become hermeneutic researchers, to explore how they [we] live
their [our] lives in interplay with others—those children for whom they
[we] care, and those adults with whom they [we] share this responsibility . . . Caregivers must become more self-aware, as well as child-
aware, and comfortable with their [our] own and the children's emo-
tionality" (pp. 88–89).

As I've done in much of this book, involving myself in this critical
reflection helps me become more aware about the far-reaching personal and professional impact of "no touch" policies. Referring to
Gilligan and Wiggins' work (1988), Leavitt suggests that as emotionally responsive caregivers, we must have "an awareness of oneself as
capable of knowing and living with the feelings of others, as able to
affect others and be affected by them" (p. 123). I feel a deep sense of
pain when I consider what it would be like for me as a preschool
teacher to not be able to change a child's diaper or not allow a child to
sit on my sit during story time. I wonder what it feels like for all of the
children and teachers whose daily experiences are influenced by similar "no touch" policies. We need to look beyond ourselves and ask
similar questions of those we say we serve, children.

Chapter 7

(Re)Claiming Touch

We could say, silence is a historical sign that is unspeakable. We could also say silence is the effect of silencing. . . . the task then is to break the silence, thereby erasing it, yet not silencing (forgetting) it.
— Maya Hostettler, *Telling the Past—Doing the Truth*

Somehow we have to try to start somewhere else, to speak, mean and write outside these limitations on what can (is possible/is allowed to) be spoken, meant and written.
— Terry Threadgold, *Feminine, Masculine and Representation*

Standing at the edge of the unthought, even the unasked, and always the unsaid, is the moment of choosing. The choice is about what is 'good,' not as an a priori form waiting to be discovered but rather as something to be wrestled with and decided upon collectively.
— Rebecca A. Martusewicz, "Say Me to Me: Desire and Education"

On November 10, 1997, National Public Radio presented a story promoting an electronic marketing tool for day-care centers and a way for parents to monitor their child's caregiver. In this story, "Day Care on the 'Net'," parents were informed they could, "Watch [their] kids playing in day care as a screen-saver on [their] computer." Among other things, the broadcast further described how some day-care centers are now using the "Watch Me" video camera system (i.e., placing video cameras in each room in the center) as an attempt to "look for ways for parents to feel relaxed" and to "make day-care teachers more accountable." The story then mentioned how the same technology is being used in home care situations, a surveillance technique referred to as "Nanny Vision." A few days later a newspaper article on the cost of high quality child care reminded the public,

A criminal background check wouldn't have weeded out Louise Woodward, 19, the British *au pair* convicted of killing the 8-month-old baby in her care. Nor would training in child care have given her the temperament to cope with a fussy baby." (Jacobs 1997, p. A16)

Two different stories sharing a common bond, they were both released immediately after nineteen-year-old nanny, Louise Woodward, was found to be guilty of killing the eight-month-old child in her charge. After the reading of the guilty verdict, parents with children in the care of a nanny suddenly found themselves also feeling guilty. These stories readily and quite easily picked up on the public's newfound anxiety and guilt, and yet another moral panic influenced public sentiment, assisting in the proliferation of "no touch" issues today.

Considering the "no touch" stories presented above and throughout this book forces me to reflect back to my earlier comments about "knowing this moral panic as a preschool teacher tormented by the hysteria of sexual abuse in child-care settings." As I have argued in other works, I no longer wish to know this torment, and I don't wish to participate in the seen and unseen hysteria currently surrounding "no touch." I refuse to allow a "sudden, relatively brief outburst of fear, concern, and anger over a given condition, threat, or behavior transform the norms and institutions of society in such a way as to make it a different place from what it was before" (Goode and Ben-Yehuda 1994, p. 226). The quality of the lives of our children and their teachers is diminished through regimes of social control like "no touch."

In his recent work, Nelson (1997) argues that "What we are historically is partly a function of what we did and said and what was done and said to and about us, along with how we responded to a host of other cultural representations" (p. 36). Critical reflection on Nelson's underlying messages influences my political actions today. Certainly as a group of people who provide a wide range of services for young children, early childhood educators, social workers, child protective service specialists, teachers, caregivers, administrators, academics, and parents have passively sat back and knowingly allowed much to be "*done and said to and about us,*" especially related to "no touch." Collectively, we have been ignorant of intellectualizing and theorizing many of the critical, underlying issues evident throughout this narrative.

Just as I did in the early 1980s, representatives of many of the groups that serve children in various capacities today are allowing their collective identities to be created, to be *marked,* by moral panic

(Edwards and Lohman 1994). The many cases presented throughout this book witness this. The growing popularity of "no touch" policies such as no-male diaper changing in child care, not allowing children to sit on caregiver laps, no hugging children on campus, and teaching caregivers how to appropriately touch/not touch children in their care, demonstrate this phenomenon.

In our drive to implement these policies, we have in effect essentially created an alibi for the truth, while we continue allowing trends like "no touch" define who we are and govern how we operate. Melton and Flood's (1994) recent work illustrates that "the field of child protection is notable more for what is not known" (p. 3). We revise ways of being with children and adults, and we change institutional (from classroom teacher-child interactions to the social worker interview) policies on the basis of untruths, while an overwhelming majority of the research reveals that child sexual abuse is most likely to occur outside our centers, away from our staff.

The relatively rare occurrence of sexual abuse in schools (in the United States, reported to occur in as few as 1 percent of all reported child sexual abuse cases in *all* schools, not just early education settings) should not define what we can and cannot do with the young children we serve as teachers and administrators (Contratto 1986). As a field we must balance the likelihood of child abuse in our centers with the costs to our profession of our overzealous prevention. What is gained by our continued support of "no touch" policy in early childhood education? Children are becoming more distrustful of adults, especially teachers; we continue to betray young children (and what we know about good early childhood practices) as we submit them to a variety of inappropriate sexual abuse curricula; caregivers are leaving the child-care profession en masse; potential talented male caregivers are looking elsewhere for employment opportunities; directors are likely to spend more money on liability than on teacher salaries; and misinformed legislators funnel millions of dollars into prevention programs that could otherwise be spent on educating our young in more effective ways (Johnson 1997b).

Moral panics use the language of epidemics to equate social ills with a medical vocabulary of causation and a moral vocabulary of motive (Blaikie 1993). The power of this medical discourse (the very same discourse which (Kempe et alia 1962) used to reveal physical abuse to the world) "lends itself to interventionist remedies focused on the individual and is a powerful tool for policy" (Howitt 1993, p. 22).

So powerful that when verbal accounts (verbal data) of child sexual abuse surfaced in the Cleveland case in England, the medical field (pediatricians) immediately sought to medicalize these verbal accounts, by gathering more scientifically reliable data (in this case subjecting children to reflex anal dilitation) to substantiate the prevalence of child sexual abuse (Collins, Kendall, and Michael 1998).

Our overreliance on these moral panics led to increasing control through "regimes of truth" (Foucault 1977). These "regimes of truth" are the "broad continuities and discontinuities in the webs of intersecting discourses . . . the theories/practices, the power-knowledges" (Middleton 1998, p. 1) which assist in defining "no touch" (Stainton Rogers and Stainton Rogers 1992; Watney 1987). Strengthening that control follows easily by making moral panics highly visible. So visible in fact, that they (un)teach all that we know about the importance of touch. This visibility assists in our dynamic construction of ignorance around "no touch," or as Felman (1997) points out, ". . . *a kind of forgetting-of forgetfulness: while learning is obviously, among other things, remembering and memorizing, ignorance is linked to what is not remembered, what will not be memorized*" (p. 25). If I, a single early childhood teacher, and we, as a collective mass of caregivers, case workers, parents, and program administrators continue to passively ignore and plead *ignorance,* then together we knowingly allow the moral panic to gain momentum, run the debate, and continue to change our nurturant and caring subjectivities (Dodd 1993). Just this past June (1998), in the wake of studies that reveal children can be pressured to make false statements while being interviewed, a judge has ordered a new trial for several teachers accused in the 1984 Fells Acres (Massachusetts) day-care center, child abuse scandal. Long after some of the most famous child sexual abuse cases (i.e., the McMartin Preschool child abuse scandal in California, or the "Cleveland affair" in England) ran their course, we continue to witness the lasting scars these cases impressed upon our collective psyche.

While moral panic has been helpful in framing much of the discussion in this book, I do not believe this construct alone necessarily helps us progress in any manner. Even though moral panic is helpful in identifying and witnessing the birth and growth of "no touch," it does not assist in moving past the death of this phenomenon. Because moral panics are said to disappear just as quickly as they appear, their representational presence can be obscured as a site of permanent struggle. Given this, "no touch" itself runs the risk of being enveloped within the disappearing moral panic, to be forgotten as quickly as it was instated. Watney (1987) believes that other theoretical models might better inform us and he feels that the replacement of moral panic with vocabulary like "representation, discourse, and the 'other'. . . bring to his work concepts drawn from fields of psychoanalysis, film studies and cultural studies to produce a deeper account of the processes of exclusion and regulation than that available in the traditional sociology of social control" (McRobbie and Thornton 1995, p. 564).

This critique is helpful for considering how far-reaching our practical and theoretical search must be in further understanding "no touch" and in seeking to present alternative ways of thinking about the institutionalization, care, and teaching of young children. Instead of simply dismissing "no touch" as only a moral panic, I can instead interrogate why "no touch" influenced me and other teachers and groups in particular ways at particular times. This interrogation might then give rise to further questions and lead us to critique, as Stephens notes, "other widespread public resonances as serious moral discourses on our time, and we might work towards developing the theoretical and methodological frameworks that would allow us to interpret the different kinds of truths embedded within contemporary discourses on threatened children" (1993, p. 251).

Within this interrogation Stephens also pleads with us to consider how much we have thought about how "no touch" affects the way children connect to one another, to caregivers and teachers, to familial cultural traditions, to local places, and to electronically mediated worlds that parents know little about.

When considering "no touch" we must implicate ourselves in the popularity of this movement. Looking back to the early part of my teaching, I can implicate myself as a preschool teacher who chose to remain silent and ignorant, allowing others to create a "pathological perception" (O'Hagan and Dillenburger 1995) of me and all male preschool teachers. After all, why else would a young male be interested in working with young children. As professionals who serve children and families in varying capacities, we must create and open up more mature, intellectual debates about the various issues in an attempt at restoring a sense of balance to our respective disciplines. We must do this instead of continuing to claim ignorance, a process "through which we construct dangerous silences, through which we legitimate their power and extend their dominion" (Silin 1994, p. 2). It is what we do with this ignorance that (mis)guides our ability to teach/learn through this process. Felman (1997) begs us to ask, "Where is the ignorance (the resistance to knowledge) located? And what can I thus learn from the locus of that ignorance?" (p. 27). How can we acknowledge it, act on it, resist, and ultimately learn from it?

Like this narrative, talking about "no touch" with pre- and inservice teachers and parents has helped me resist ignorance and become more active, as the stories I share assist me and others in "moving out of a silence . . . shaping a new public language, generating communities to receive and disseminate them on a global scale, ultimately creating more and mores spaces for them to be heard" (Plummer 1996, p. 45). This sharing helps give me the strength to face the past, face the present, and "face the unspeakable things unspoken" (Hostettler 1996, p. 413). As part of the process of "moving out of a silence," stories of transgression, of desire, and of the erotic, might then replace or at least be critically read alongside the traditional, rational humanist stories that dominate historical and current early education professional discourse (hooks 1994; Phelan 1993; Tobin 1997; Todd 1997). Recognizing that there are many "no touch" issues that we cannot tolerate knowing (Britzman 1998) without then acting on them, these new stories could help in the further interrogation of these critical issues.

Theorizing and Teaching Alternative Stories of Touch

Because my recent work has been so heavily entangled with "no touch," I've actively sought out, heard, and studied many more stories focused around this theme in the past few years. One attempt to move beyond that is by researching and sharing alternative stories, like those presented in chapter 4—stories that illustrate how many early childhood professionals have sought to counter the "no touch" theme in their own work. This is an attempt to enact what Carter (1993) challenges teacher educators to ask of themselves: "Have we authored our work in such a way that lives have changed for the better, most importantly, the lives of children, who are . . . hard at the work of creating their own *very* important educational stories?" (p. 11).

Addressing Carter's plea, we need to increasingly ask of ourselves and of the respective academic and institutional disciplines we occupy, what kinds of new, alternative narratives might we personally author, might we construct, replicate, and share in "such a way that lives have changed for the better." An example that immediately comes to mind is that of the Touch Research Institute (TRI) in Miami. This institute is actively responding to the lack of critical basic and applied research on the effects of "no touch" on children and caregivers (Daro 1991; Isbell and Morrow 1991; Melton and Flood 1994). For example, researchers at TRI are currently studying how an elementary education professional development program enhances touch in classrooms. The study includes inservice sessions that focus on how to enhance touch, as part of a model for reintroducing touch in the same school system that recently mandated a "no touch" policy.

Like TRI, our own inquiry could follow the multiple paths Bredbeck (1995) describes, as either "activist" (seeks to change a system) or "pure" (seeks to expose a system in its entirety as a system) critique, while we seek to intellectually address and change current "no touch" policies. This intellectual engagement would take place in close juxtaposition to historical narratives, with the past always present. In this process we are then always "remembering and rerembering things past" (Hostettler 1996, p. 415) as we continually progress, constructing new identities and new meanings as new possibilities arise (Brunner 1996).

Another perspective would be to think of the different types of new conditions in our practice(s) that we can acknowledge, that make it possible to rethink touch (Felman 1997). These new conditions, or new narratives, could mark an "emotional moving forward." In this active stance, we become more "defiant . . . [we] complain [we] yell" (Abbott 1989, p. 39) about what we've witnessed and in regard to how we plan to move forward. Just as Erica McWilliam's recent work reminds us, we have to ask:

> What then might be possible for teachers who claim all pedagogical space, including the virtual, as an erotic field where 'volatile' bodies can and do engage intimately and productively with each other in a giddy and fumbling embrace? What uncanny, irregular, and powerful productions of knowledge might a radical pedagogy then be able to generate? How contagious might we be? (1997, p. 230)

These once untold political stories of transgression, desire, and of the erotic, might then help to redefine or (re)position what it means to be a teacher of young children; what it means to be a child protective services case-worker who makes a critical decision to remove children from their home and place them in foster care; what it feels like to be the only male staff in a child-care center; what a high school sexual education curriculum should read like in the age of AIDS; and how college instructors teach early childhood caregivers and teachers about child sexuality. Our critical questioning of popular assumptions embedded in "no touch" policies would then assist us in creating alternative narratives that could assist us in "moving out of a silence." Here is where our struggle must begin.

Appendix

Morning Edition (NPR) January 4, 1994
Transcript #1252 Segment #6
"Day Care Center Goes to Extremes to Protect Reputation"
BOB EDWARDS, Host: Whether the target is a pop star, such as Michael Jackson, a Catholic bishop, or someone out of the public eye, allegations of child abuse, particularly sexual abuse, always get our attention. Such allegations have become so common in American society that people who work with children cannot help but react. Even as they struggle to protect children from abuse, they try to protect themselves against liability. Experts say the precautions being taken at some day care centers go too far, and the children pay for it. From member station WBUR in Boston, Tovia Smith reports.

[snack time in day care center]

TOVIA SMITH, Reporter: It's snack time just after school. A day care teacher is loading up the paper plates in front of a dozen hungry preschoolers.

DAY CARE TEACHER: Everyone get cookies?

CHILD: Yes.

2nd CHILD: Yes.

DAY CARE TEACHER: All right, you guys, get in here.

[children laughing]

SMITH: A little boy with dark wide eyes watches an Oreo cookie submerge in a plastic cup of orange juice. There are giggles all around. This is a close bunch. Teachers describe it as a big family, but there are very strict rules here as to how this family interacts.

JOAN TANNER, Director, Upper Falls Children's Center: It's against
our policy to pick up the kids. It's against our policy to
hold them on your lap.

SMITH: Joan Tanner is director of the Upper Falls Children's
Center in Newton. If the policies here seem strict, she
says, it's because the stakes are high.

TANNER: The doors have to be open, and not one teacher is
allowed to be alone with one child in the room behind
a closed door, because I know just from knowing about
the sexual abuse cases that are in the newspaper and
stuff, that's how it's happened.

SMITH: To keep it from happening here, Tanner requires extensive background checks and references for all employees. She's confident that the teachers she's hired
are trustworthy. The "no-touch" policy, she says, is
more to protect the center than the children. In the
business of day care, Tanner explains, reputation is
everything, and reputation is fragile. It would be too
easy, she says, for one innocent hug or playful piggyback ride to be misinterpreted.

TANNER: The picking-up thing, I just—I don't allow, because
that's one of those issues where you have, you know,
the direct physical contact, body to body, that could
be misconstrued, so I—I stop it there.

SMITH: And stop it often. Tanner says she's constantly remind-
ing both staffers and kids to keep their distance.

TANNER: I'll say, "No. No holding." Or, if it's one of the little
kids, I might say, "OK, Steven, now you know you
need to get down," and then I will privately remind
the person, "Remember, now, we don't do that. I know
you're just enjoying this child, however, it could be
misconstrued. It could be a problem for you."

SMITH: Policies differ among day care centers, but more and
more early childhood educators are being trained to
err on the side of distance rather than risk false accu-
ation. This day care worker, who works in Central
Massachusetts, says she got her first warning even
before her first job.

DAY CARE WORKER: In college they trained us to have the child
beside us, not on our lap, when we're reading books

and what not, and not to give them that hug or kiss for fear that a parent will walk in and see this, or that some sort of instructor will come in and call us in that we're touching these children in ways that we shouldn't be.

Dr. CYNTHIA CROSSENTOWER, Author, *Secret Scars*: People are scared, people are frightened, and so I think that a lot of schools are making the decision to protect themelves, you know, and I think that it's really too bad.

SMITH: Dr. Cynthia Crossentower is author of *Secret Scars*. She says decisions that may be good for day care facilities may not be good for kids.

CROSSENTOWER: Touching is an integral part of learning, and sometimes we need the proverbial and literal pat on the back.

SMITH: Or even kiss on the cheek. This mother, whose daughter is in public school in Central Massachusetts, says she became furious when she found how teachers reacted when her daughter fell off a slide at school.

ANGRY MOTHER: I saw my mother, I'd say, maybe three hours after it had happened. I went home from work, and the first thing my daughter said to me was, "The teacher didn't hug me or kiss my boo-boo." And it's like cold fish. Nobody is willing to hug. When she's sad, she has to deal with that herself. There's not that little extra hug there.

SMITH: That little extra hug, however, at day care and at home, is important not only to a child's emotional or psychological well-being, but also to a kid's physical growth and development.

Dr. TIFFANY FIELD, Director, Touch Research Institute: [on telephone] Basically, every function you can think of is affected by touch.

SMITH: Dr. Tiffany Field is director of the Touch Research Institute at the University of Miami's School of Medicine.

FIELD: We know that children need touch to grow. We know that they need it for their immune system. Children who aren't touched have much more illness, in addition to failing to thrive. You know, it highlights how critical it is for health and for growth, and, actually, for learning as well.

SMITH: While it's understandable that a day care center would be concerned about liability, even attorneys who specialize in child abuse cases consider a no-touch policy an over-reaction. It is prudent, lawyers say, to always keep a second teacher around, just like a male obstetrician who will only do examinations in the presence of a nurse. But, attorney Thomas Lynch, past chairman of the Boston Bar Association's Tort Committee, says prohibiting all touch may be going too far.

THOMAS LYNCH, Attorney: I think that at some point defensive practice, whether it's in the field of medicine or, in this case, child care, crosses a line where the defensive practice tends to detract from what the ultimate purpose of what you're doing is. And, in this case, if the interaction of appropriate and legitimate touching is taken away, then it seems to me you're taking away from the quality of the day care you're giving.

DAY CARE TEACHER: Good game today, guys. When we have finished snacks, we'll be going to the gym.

3rd CHILD: Yay!
4th CHILD: Yay!
5th CHILD: Yay!
6th CHILD: Super-yay!

SMITH: Day care director Joan Tanner says she does worry about her hands-off policy and how it may affect the kids at her center, but she also worries about the more immediate threat of a lawsuit.

TANNER: You know, it's a difficult situation for me because I'm the huggy sort of a person. I think it's unfortunate that we have to be so concerned along these lines, but we obviously do have to be so concerned.

SMITH: But, if the concern is about sexual abuse some psychologists say a no-touch policy is exactly the wrong reaction. They worry it will send kids the confusing and unhealthy message that any and all touch is bad. Others say kids who don't get the touch they need from adults, may seek it out elsewhere. Ironically, says one psychologist, one of the best ways for parents to protect their kids from becoming victims of sexual abuse may be to make sure the kids get plenty of touch that's healthy and nurturing.

For National Public Radio, this is Tovia Smith in Boston.

References

Abbott, Steve. 1989. *View askew: Postmodern investigations*. San Francisco: Androgyne Books.

Adkins, Lisa, and Vicki Merchant. 1996. Introduction to *Sexualizing the social: Power and the organization of sexuality*, by L. Adkins and V. Merchant. New York: St. Martin's Press.

Adler, Jerry. 1994. Kids growing up scared. *Newsweek*, 10 January, 43–50.

Alanen, Leena. 1994. Gender and generation: Feminism and the "child question." In *Childhood matters: Social theory, practice and politics*, edited by J. Qvortrup, M. Bardy, G. Sgritta, and H. Wintersberger. Hong Kong: Avebury.

Albers, Eric. 1991. Child sexual abuse programs. *Child and Adolescent Social Work* 8:117–125.

Altman, Dennis. 1995. Political sexualities: Meanings and identities in the time of AIDS. In *Conceiving sexuality: Approaches to sex research in a postmodern world*, edited by R. Parker and J. Gagnon. London: Routledge.

Annin, Peter. 1996. Superpredators arrive: Should we cage the new breed of vicious kids? *Newsweek*, 22 January, 57.

Appelbaum, David. 1988. *The interpenetrating reality: Bringing the body to touch*. New York: Peter Lang.

Bantick, Christopher. 1997. Fathers and children. *The Courier-Mail*. 10 April.

Batchelor, Ervin S., R. S. Dean, S. Raymond, B. Gridley, and B. Batchelor. 1990. Reports of child sexual abuse in schools. *Psychology in the Schools, 27*:131–137.

Beck, Ulrick. 1992. *Risk society: Towards a new modernity.* Translated by Mark Ritter. Thousand Oaks: Sage.

Becket, Lori. 1996. "Where do you draw the line?" Education and sexual identities. In *Schooling and sexualities: Teaching for a positive sexuality,* edited by L. Laskey and C. Beavis. Victoria: Deakin Centre for Education and Change.

Bennett, Peter. 1979. *The illustrated child.* New York: G. P. Putnam Son's.

Berliner, Lucy. 1997. Foreword to *Understanding child molesters: Taking charge,* by Eric Leberg. Thousand Oaks: Sage.

Berrick, Jill D., and Neil Gilbert. 1991. *With the best intentions: The child sexual abuse prevention movement.* New York: Guilford Press.

Blaikie, Andrew. 1993. *Illegitimacy, sex, and society: Northeast Scotland, 1750–1900.* Oxford: Clarendon Press.

Bogat, G. Anne, and Marianne P. McGrath. 1993. Preschoolers' cognitions of authority, and its relationship to sexual abuse education. *Child Abuse & Neglect, 17*:651–662.

Borkin, Joyce, and Lesley Frank. 1986. Sexual abuse prevention for preschoolers: A pilot program. *Child Welfare, 115*:75–82.

Boyle, Sarah. 1997. Introduction to *Sexual abuse—the child's voice: Poppies on the rubbish heap,* by Madge Bray. Bristol, PA: Jessica Kingsley Publishers.

Brant, Clare, and Yun Lee Too. 1994. Introduction to *Rethinking sexual harassment,* by C. Brant and Y. L. Too. Boulder: Pluto Press.

Brazelton, Terry B. 1984. Introduction to *The many facets of touch,* edited by C. Brown. Skillman, NJ: Johnson & Johnson Baby Products Company.

Bredbeck, Gregory W. 1995. The new queer narrative: Intervention and critique. *Textual Practice, 9*:477–502.

Breiner, Sandra J. 1990. *Slaughter of the innocents: Child abuse through the ages and today.* London: Plenum Press.

Brettell, Caroline B. 1993. Introduction: Fieldwork, text, and audience. In *When they read what we write: The politics of ethnography,* edited by C. B. Brettell. Connecticut: Bergin & Garvey.

Brinton, Connie, and Tom Heinrich. 1997. Now that Hawaii has Megan's Law . . . It gives a false security. *The Honolulu Advertiser.* 20 July.

Bristow, Joseph. 1997. *Sexuality.* New York: Routledge.

Britzman, Deborah P. 1998. *Lost subjects, contested objects: Toward a psychoanalytic inquiry of learning.* New York: State University of New York Press.

Brook, Stephen, and Katherine Glascott. 1997. Education chief backs classroom abuse watchdog. *The Australian.* 20 February.

Brunner, Diane D. 1996. Silent bodies: Miming those killing norms of gender. *JCT:*9–15.

Bryson, Anne. 1996. *Broadside.* New South Wales: Community Child Care Co-operative Ltd.

Carrington, Kerry, and Anna Bennett. 1996. "Girls' mags" and the pedagogical formation of the girl. In *Feminisms and pedagogies of everyday life,* edited by C. Luke. New York: State University of New York Press.

Carson, Joan C., and Dudley Sykes. 1991. *Behaviors of preschoolers and their teachers: Little children draw big circles.* Springfield, IL: Charles C. Thomas.

Carter, Kathy. 1993. The place of story in the study of teaching and teacher education. *Educational Researcher, 22:*5–12, 18.

Casey, Kathleen. 1993. *I answer with my life: Life histories of women teachers working for social change.* New York: Routledge.

Casper, Virginia, H. K. Cuffaro, S. Schultz, J. G. Silin, and E. Wickens. 1996. Toward a most thorough understanding of the world: Sexual orientation and early childhood education. *Harvard Educational Review, 66:*271–293.

Center on the Family. 1995. *Hawaii kids count.* Honolulu: University of Hawaii.

Chadwick, David L. 1994. A response to "The impact of 'moral panic' on professional behavior in cases of child sexual abuse". *Journal of Child Sexual Abuse, 3*:127–131.

Cheeseman, Brian. 1994. Media representations of children, childhood and their play culture in the post-James Bulger case period. Paper presented at the Annual World Conference on the Right for Children to Play, East Asia/Pacific Regional Conference Hong Kong.

Clough, Patricia T. 1992. *The end(s) of ethnography: From realism to social criticism.* London: Sage.

Coddington, Deborah. 1997. *The Australian paedophile and sex offender index.* Sydney: PSI Index.

Cohen, Stanley. 1972. *Folk devils and moral panics: The creation of the Mods and Rockers.* Oxford: Martin Robertson.

————. 1973. Sensitization: The case of the Mods and Rockers. In *The manufacture of news: Social problems, deviance and the mass media*, edited by S. Cohen and J. Young. Beverly Hills: Sage.

Collins, Alan, G. Kendall, and M. Michael. 1998. Resisting a diagnostic technique: The case of reflex anal dilatation. *Sociology of Health & Illness, 20*:1–28.

Colt, George H. 1997. The magic of touch: Massage's healing powers make it serious medicine. *Life*, August, 52–62.

Connell, Robert W., and Gary W. Dowsett, eds. 1992. *Rethinking sex: Social theory and sexuality research.* Melbourne: Melbourne University Press.

Conte, Jon R., and Linda A. Fogarty. 1990. Sexual abuse prevention programs for children. *Education and Urban Society, 22*:270–284.

Conte, Jon R., C. Rosen, and L. Saperstein. 1986. An analysis of programs to prevent the sexual victimization of children. *Journal of Primary Prevention, 6*:142–155.

Contratto, Susan. 1986. Child abuse and the politics of care. *Journal of Education, 168*:70–79.

Corbett, Susan. 1991. Children and sexuality. *Young Children, 46*: 71–77.

Daro, Deborah. 1991. Child sexual abuse prevention: Separating fact from fiction. *Child Abuse & Neglect, 15*:1–4.

Davies, Bronwyn. 1994. Beyond dualism and towards multiple subjectivities. In *Texts of desire*, edited by L. K. Christian-Smith. Washington, DC: Falmer Press.

Delandshere, Ginette, and Anthony R. Petrosky. 1994. Capturing teachers' knowledge: Perfomance assessment, a) and poststructuralist epistemology, b) from a post-structuralist perspective, c) and post-structuralism, d) none of the above. *Educational Researcher, 23*:11–18.

Del Prete, Toni. 1997. Hands off? The touchy subject of touching. *The Education Digest, 62*:59–61.

deMause, Lloyd. 1974. *The history of childhood*. New York: The Psychohistory Press.

deYoung, Mary. 1988. The good touch/bad touch dilemma. *Child Welfare, 67*:60–68.

Dilg, Mary A. 1997. Why I am a multiculturalist: The power of stories told and untold. *English Journal, 86*:64–69.

Dittman, Laura L. 1986. Finding the best care for your infant or toddler. *Young Children, 41*:43–46.

Dodd, Phillip. 1993. Moral panic: The sequel. *Sight and Sound, 3*:3.

Dollimore, John. 1991. *Sexual dissidence: Augustine to Wilde, Freud to Foucault*. Oxford: Clarendon Press.

Douglas, Tom. 1995. *Scapegoats: Transferring blame*. New York: Routledge.

Duggan, Lisa. 1995. Sex panics. In *Sex wars: Sexual dissent and political culture*, edited by L. Duggan and N. D. Hunter. New York: Routledge.

Duncan, Judith. 1998. New Zealand kindergarten teachers and sexual abuse protection policies. Unpublished manuscript.

Durham, Martin. 1997. Conservative agendas and government policy. In *New sexual agendas*, edited by L. Segal. New York: New York University Press.

Economist. 1993. State of the nation: Moral panic. *The Economist*, 27 February, *326*:62.

———. 1996. Britain: Delinquent behavior. *The Economist*, 2 November, *241*:57–58.

Edwards, Susan M., and Jacqueline S. Lohman. 1994. The impact of "moral panic" on professional behavior in cases of child abuse: An international perspective. *Journal of Child Sexual Abuse*, *3*:103–126.

Eisen, Vitka, and Irene Hall. 1996. Introduction to special issue on lesbian, gay, bisexual, and transgender people and education. *Harvard Education Review*, *66*:i–ix.

Elrod, Jeanne M., and Roger H. Rubin. 1993. Parental involvement in sexual abuse prevention education. *Child Abuse & Neglect*, *17*:527–538.

Etaugh, Claire, and Spencer A. Rathus. 1995. *The world of children*. Forth Worth: Harcourt Brace, Jovanovich.

Fass, Paula S. 1997. *Kidnapped: Child abduction in America*. London: Oxford University Press.

Felman, Shoshana. 1997. Psychoanalysis and education: Teaching terminable and interminable. In *Learning desire: Perspectives on pedagogy, culture, and the unsaid*, edited by S. Todd. New York: Routledge.

Field, Tiffany. 1990. *Infancy*. Cambridge: Harvard University Press.

Finkelhor, David, L. M. Williams, and N. Burns. 1988. *Nursery crimes: Sexual abuse in day care*. Newbury Park, CA: Sage.

Fish, Stanley. 1980. *Is there a text in this class? The authority of interpretive communities*. Cambridge, MA: Harvard University Press.

Fossey, Richard, and Todd DeMitchell. 1995. Let the master respond: Should schools be strictly liable when employees sexually abuse children? Paper presented at the Annual American Education Research Association Conference, San Francisco, CA.

Foucault, Michel. 1977. *Discipline and punish: The birth of the prison.* London: Allen Lane.

——. 1980. Power/knowledge: Selected interviews and other writings 1972–1977. (C. Gordon, ed.) New York: Pantheon.

——. 1981. The order of discourse. In *Untying the text: A post structuralist reader,* edited by R. Young. Boston: Routledge and Kegan Paul.

——. 1984a. What is enlightenment? In *The Foucault reader,* edited by P. Rabinow. New York: Pantheon Books.

——. 1984b. Nietzsche, genealogy, history. In *The Foucault reader,* edited by P. Rabinow. New York: Pantheon Books.

Fout, John C., ed. 1992. *Forbidden history: The state, society, and the regulation of sexuality in modern Europe.* Chicago: The University of Chicago Press.

Freeman-Longo, Robert E. 1996. Feel good legislation: Prevention or calamity. *Child Abuse & Neglect, 20*:95–101.

Fryer, George E. 1993. *Child abuse and the social environment.* San Francisco: Westview Press.

Gagnon, John H., and Richard G. Parker. 1995. Conceiving sexuality. In *Conceiving sexuality: Approaches to sex research in a postmodern world,* edited by R. Parker and J. Gagnon. London: Routledge.

Garber, Marjorie. 1995. *Vice versa: Bisexuality and the eroticism of everyday life.* London: Hamish Hamilton.

Gilbert, Neil. 1988. Teaching children to prevent sexual abuse. *Public Interest, 93*:3–15.

——. 1991. The phantom epidemic of sexual assault. *Public Interest, 103*:54–65.

Gilligan, Carol, and G. Wiggins. 1988. The origins of morality in early childhood relationships. In *Mapping the moral domain,* edited by C. Gilligan, J. Ward, J. Taylor, and B. Bardige. MA: Harvard University Press.

Giroux, Henry. 1996. Foreword to *Poststructuralism, politics and education,* by Michael Peters. Westport, CT: Bergin & Garvey.

Goode, Erich, and Nachman Ben-Yehuda. 1994. *Moral panics: The social construction of deviance.* Oxford: Blackwell.

Gramsci, Antonio. 1980. Selections from the prison notebooks of Antonio Gramsci. Ed. and trans. Q. Hogue and G.N. Smith. New York: International Publishers.

Grosz, Elizabeth. 1994. Animal sex: Libido as desire and death. In *Sexy bodies: The strange carnalities of feminism,* edited by E. Grosz and E. Probyn. London: Routledge.

———. 1995. *Space, time and perversion: Essays on the politics of bodies.* London: Routledge.

Grosz, Elizabeth, and Elspeth Probyn. 1994. Introduction to *Sexy bodies: The strange carnalities of feminism,* by E. Grosz and E. Probyn. London: Routledge.

Hall, Stuart, C. Critcher, T. Jefferson, J. Clarke, and B. Roberts. 1978. *Policing the crisis: Mugging, the state, and law and order.* New York: Holmes & Meier Publishers, Inc.

Haste, Helen. 1994. *The sexual metaphor.* Cambridge: Harvard University Press.

Hawaii Teacher Standards Board. 1998. Available from http://www.hsta.org/tsb/tsbbill.html.

Haywood, Chris. 1996. "Out of the curriculum": Sex talking, talking sex. *Curriculum Studies,* 4:229–249.

Heller, Scott. 1996. Visual images replace text as focal point for many scholars. *Chronicle of Higher Education,* 19 July A8–A15.

———. 1998. Childhood: The meaning of children in culture becomes a focal point for scholars. *Chronicle of Higher Education,* 7 August A14–A16.

Heller, Sharon. 1997. *The vital touch.* New York: Henry Holt.

Hendrick, Harry. 1997. Constructions and reconstructions of British childhood: An interpretive survey, 1800 to the present. In *Constructing and reconstructing childhood: Contemporary issues in the sociological study of childhood,* edited by A. James & A. Prout. Washington, DC: Falmer Press.

Hendrick, Joanne. 1996. *The whole child: Developmental education for the early years.* Columbus: Merrill.

———. 1997. *Total learning: Curriculum for the young child.* Columbus: Merrill.

Henriques, Julian, W. Holloway, C. Urwin, C. Venn, and V. Walkerdine. 1984. *Changing the subject: Psychology, social regulation and subjectivity.* London: Methuen.

Hildebrand, Verna. 1986a. *Guiding young children.* NJ: Simon & Schuster.

———. 1986b. *Introduction to early childhood education.* New York: Macmillan.

Hollander, Sheila K. 1992. Making young children aware of sexual abuse. *Elementary School Guidance & Counseling, 26*:305–317.

Holt, John. 1975. *Escape from childhood.* London: Penguin.

Honig, Alice S. 1989. Quality infant/toddler caregiving: Are there magic recipes? *Young Children, 44*:4–10.

hooks, bell. 1994. *Teaching to transgress: Education as the practice of freedom.* New York: Routledge.

Hostettler, Maya. 1996. Telling the past—doing the truth: Toni Morrison's *Beloved. Women's History Review,* 5:401–416

Howitt, Dennis. 1993. *Child abuse errors: When good intentions go wrong.* New Brunswick: Rutgers University Press.

Hunt, Ros. 1994. Seventy times seven? Forgiveness and sexual violence in Christian pastoral care. In *Rethinking sexual harassment,* edited by C. Brant and Y. L. Too. Boulder: Pluto Press.

Hyson, Marion C., L. C. Whitehead, and C. M. Prudhoe. 1988. Influences on attitudes toward physical affection between adults and children. *Early Childhood Research Quarterly, 3*:55–75.

Irvine, Janice M. 1995. *Sexuality education across cultures: Working with differences.* San Francisco: Jossey-Bass.

Isbell, Rebecca, and Brent Morrow. 1991. Should young children be asked to protect themselves? *Childhood Education,* 67:252–253.

Jacobs, Joanne. 1997. Forget "high-quality, low-cost" care. *The Honolulu Advertiser*, 5 November.

Jameson, Frederick. 1986. On magic realism in film. *Critical Inquiry*, 12:301–326.

Jenkins, Philip. 1992. *Intimate enemies: Moral panic in contemporary Great Britain*. New York: Aldine de Gruyter.

Jenks, Chris. 1996. *Childhood*. New York: Routledge.

Jóhannesson, Ingólfur A. 1998. Genealogy and progressive politics: Reflections on the notion of usefulness. In *Foucault's challenge: Discourse, knowledge, and power in education*, edited by T. Popkewitz and M. Brennan. New York: Teachers College Press.

Johnson, Richard. 1996. Sexual dissonances: Or the "impossibility" of sexual education. *Curriculum Studies*, 4:163–189.

———. 1997. Contested borders, contingent lives: An introduction. In *Border patrols: Policing the boundaries of heterosexuality*, edited by D. L. Steinberg, D. Epstein, and R. Johnson. London: Cassell.

Johnson, Richard T. 1995. *The missing discourses of pleasure and desire in early education*. Paper presented at the Annual Meeting of the American Educational Research Association, San Francisco, CA.

———. 1997a. "No touch" policy in early schooling: Now we can't touch children anymore. *Educating Young Children: Learning and Teaching in the Early Childhood Years*, 3:10–15.

———. 1997b. The "no touch" policy. In *Making a place for pleasure in early childhood education*, edited by J. Tobin. New Haven: Yale University Press.

———. 1997c. "No touch" policies and the erasure of physical relationships in primary schooling. *Perspectives on Educational Leadership*, 7:3.

———. 1997d. "No touch" policies and the erasure of sexuality in early education. Paper presented at Children's Rights: The Next Step-Australian Conference on Children's Rights, Brisbane, Queensland.

————. 1997e. Touching children: A valid part of the educational process or not? Paper presented at the Queensland Institute for Educational Administration Conference on "The Legal, Social and Long-term Learning Costs of the 'No-Touch' Policy in Education," Brisbane, Queensland.

Joint Commission of the Chancellor and the Special Commissioner. 1994. *Prevention of child abuse: Final report.* (ERIC Document Reproduction Service No. Ed 378 521).

Jones, Stanley E. 1994. *The right touch: Understanding and using the language of physical contact.* Cresskill, NJ: Hampton Press, Inc.

Katz, David. 1989. *The world of touch.* Translated by L. E. Krueger. Hillsdale, NJ: Lawrence Erlbaum Associates.

Kelly, Susan J., R. Brant and J. Waterman. 1993. Sexual abuse of children in day care centers. *Child Abuse & Neglect, 17*:71–89.

Kelly, Ursula. 1997. *Schooling desire: Literacy, cultural politics, and pedagogy.* New York: Routledge.

Kempe, Henry, F. Silverman, B. Steele, W. Droegemueller, and M. Silver. 1962. The battered child syndrome. *JAMA, 181*:17–21.

Kenway, Jane. 1996. Foreword *Schooling and sexualities: Teaching for a positive sexuality,* edited by L. Laskey and C. Beavis. Victoria: Deakin Centre for Education and Change.

Kitzinger, Jennie. 1997. Who are you kidding? Children, power and the struggle against sexual abuse. In *Constructing and reconstructing childhood: Contemporary issues in the sociological study of childhood,* edited by A. James and A. Prout. Washington, DC: Falmer Press.

Klaus, Marshall H., and John H. Kennell. 1976. *Maternal-infant bonding: The impact of early separation or loss on family development.* Saint Louis: Mosby.

Klein, Susan S. 1992. Why should we care about gender and sexuality in the education? In *Sexuality and the curriculum: The politics and practices of sexuality education,* edited by J. Sears. New York: Teachers College Press.

Krivascka, James J. 1989. Your first step in preventing abuse: Look critically at prepackaged programs. *American School Board Journal, 176*:35–57.

Kronholz, June. 1998. Teachers face need to avoid kids' hugs. *Honolulu Star Bulletin,* 29 May.

LaForge, Ann E. 1994. World-wise babycare. *Child,* 15 April, 67–69.

Lather, Patti. 1991. *Feminist research in education: Within/against.* Geelong, Australia: Deakin University Press.

Leavitt, Robyn L. 1994. *Power and emotion in infant-toddler daycare.* New York: State University of New York Press.

Leberg, Eric. 1997. *Understanding child molesters: Taking charge.* Thousand Oaks: Sage.

Lees, Sue. 1993. *Sugar and spice: Sexuality and adolescent girls.* London: Penguin.

Lewis, Jill. 1997. "So how did your condom use go last night, daddy?" Sex talk and daily life. In *New sexual agendas,* edited by L. Segal. New York: New York University Press.

Lindstrom, Lamont. 1990. Knowledge and power in a South Pacific society. Honolulu: University of Hawaii Press.

Lively, Virginia, and Edwin Lively. 1991. *Sexual development of young children.* Albany: Delmar.

Lumsden, Linda S. 1992. Stemming the tide of child sexual abuse: The role schools can play. *Oregon School Study Council, 35*:1–53.

Maclean, Hunter. 1997. Disturbing new figures about child abuse. *Macleans, 110*:15.

Madus, Jill L. 1995. *Unstable bodies: Victorian representations of sexuality and maternity.* New York: St. Martin's Press.

Martusewicz, Rebecca A. 1997. Say me to me: Desire and education. In *Learning desire: Perspectives on pedagogy, culture, and the unsaid,* edited by S. Todd. New York: Routledge.

Mayden, Bronwyn. 1996. Child sexual abuse: Teen pregnancy's silent partner. *Children's Voice, 5*:28–29.

Mazur, Sally, and Carrie Pekor. 1985. Can teachers touch children anymore? Physical contact and its value in child development. *Young Children, 40*:10–12.

McCormick, Naomi B. 1994. *Sexual salvation: Affirming women's sexual rights and pleasures.* London: Praeger.

McEvoy, Alan W. 1990. Child abuse law and school policy. *Education and Urban Society, 22*:247–257.

McLeod, Nancy S., and Cheryl Wright. 1996. Developmentally appropriate criteria for evaluating sexual abuse prevention programs. *Early Childhood Education Journal, 24*:71–75.

McNay, Lois. 1991. The Foucaultian body and the exclusion of experience. *Hypatia, 6*:125–139.

McRobbie, Angela, and Sarah L. Thornton. 1995. Rethinking "moral panic" for multi-mediated social worlds. *British Journal of Sociology, 46*:559–574.

McWilliam, Erica. 1996. Touchy subjects: A risky inquiry into pedagogical pleasure. *British Educational Research Journal, 22*:305–317.

———. 1997. Beyond the missionary position: Teacher desire and radical pedagogy. In *Learning desire: Perspectives on pedagogy, culture, and the unsaid,* edited by S. Todd. New York: Routledge.

Melson, Gail F., A. Fogel, and D. R. Powell. 1988. The development of nurturance in young children. *Young Children, 43*:57–65.

Melton, Gary B., and Mary F. Flood. 1994. Research policy and child maltreatment: Developing the scientific foundation for effective protection of children. *Child Abuse & Neglect, 18*:1–28.

Middleton, Sue. 1998. *Disciplining sexuality: Foucault, life histories, and education.* New York: Teachers College Press.

Mikkelsen, Edwin. J. 1997. Responding to allegations of sexual abuse in child care and early childhood education programs. *Young Children, 52*:47–51.

Millet, Kate. 1984. Beyond politics? Children and sexuality. In *Pleasure and danger: Exploring female sexuality,* edited by C. Vance. Melbourne: Routledge.

Money, John. 1995. *Gendermaps: Social constructionism, feminism, and sexosophical history.* New York: Continuum.

Montagu, Ashley. 1978. *Touching: The human significance of the skin.* San Francisco, CA: Harper & Row.

Morrison, George, S. 1995. *Early childhood education today.* Columbus: Prentice Hall.

Moss, Gemma. 1993. In *Texts of desire: Essays on fiction, femininity and schooling,* edited by L. K. Christian-Smith. Washington, DC: Falmer Press.

Murray, Teresa, and Michael McClure. 1996. *Moral panic: Exposing the religious right's agenda on sexuality.* London: Cassell.

National Public Radio. 1997 "Day care on the 'Net'," 10 November, 1997, <http://www.npr.org/ramfiles/971110.atc2.03.ram.> (10 November, 1997).

Nelson, Cary. 1997. *Manifestations of a tenured radical.* New York: New York University Press.

Newman, Lucile F., and Stephen Buka. 1991. *Every child a learner: Reducing risks of learning impairment during pregnancy and infancy* (Report No. SI-90-9). Education Commission of the States, Denver, CO.

Nowesnick, Mary. 1993. Shattered lives. *The American School Board Journal, 180*:14–19.

O'Chee, Amanda. 1997. Sex-charge fears put men on the outer. *The Courier-Mail,* 28 January.

O'Hagan, Kieran, and Karola Dillenburger. 1995. *The abuse of women within childcare work.* Philadelphia: Open University Press.

O'Loughlin, Michael. 1997. Imagining a socially just and racially inclusive psychology: Musing from post-colonial theory. Paper presented at the Fifth European Congress of Psychology, University College Dublin, Dublin, Ireland.

O'Neill, Helen. 1997. Suspicious minders. *The Australian,* 27 February.

Pally, Marcia. 1994. *Sex and sensibility: Reflections on forbidden mirrors and the will to censor.* Hopewell, NJ: ECCO Press.

Phelan, Peggy. 1993. *Unmarked: The politics of performance.* New York: Routledge.

Platt, Steve. 1995. Moral panic. *New Statesman & Society, 8*:14–16.

Plummer, Ken. 1995. *Telling sexual stories: Power, change and social worlds.* New York: Routledge.

———. 1996. Intimate citizenship and the culture of sexual story telling. In *Sexual cultures: Communities, values and intimacy,* edited by J. Weeks and J. Holland. New York: St. Martin's Press.

Pratt, John. 1997. "This is not a prison": Foucault, the Panopticon and Pentonville. In *Foucault: The legacy,* edited by C. O'Farrell. Queensland: Queensland University of Technology.

Purkiss, Dianne. 1994. The lecherous professor revisited: Plato, pedagogy and the scene of harassment. In *Rethinking sexual harassment,* edited by C. Brant and Y. L. Too. Boulder: Pluto Press.

Qvortrup, Jens. 1994. Childhood matters: An introduction. In *Childhood matters: Social theory, practice and politics,* edited by J. Qvortrup, M. Bardy, G. Sgritta, and H. Wintersberger. Hong Kong: Avebury.

Ramelli, Adriana. 1997. Now that Hawaii has Megan's Law . . . We'll all be safer. *The Honolulu Advertiser,* 20 July.

Rhedding-Jones, Jeanette. 1996. Researching early schooling: Poststructural practices and academic writing in an ethnography. *British Journal of Sociology of Education, 17*:21–37.

Richter, Alan. 1987. *The language of sexuality.* London: McFarland & Company, Inc.

Robertson, Judith. 1997. Fantasy's confines: Popular culture and the education of the female primary-school teacher. In *Learning desire: Perspectives on pedagogy, culture, and the unsaid,* edited by S. Todd. New York: Routledge.

Rose, Nikolas. 1990. *Governing the soul: The shaping of the private self.* New York: Routledge.

Rothbaum, Fred, A. Grauer, and D. J. Rubin. 1997. Becoming sexual: Differences between child and adult sexuality. *Young Children, 52*:22–28.

Scafidi, Frank A., T. Field, A. Wheeden, S. Schanberg, C. Kuhn, R. Symanski, E. Zimmerman, and E. Bandstra. 1996. Cocaine-exposed preterm neonates show behavioral and hormonal differences. *Pediatrics, 97*:851–855.

Schorsch, Anita. 1979. *Images of childhood: An illustrated social history.* New York: Mayflower Books.

Segal, Lynne. 1997. Preface to *New sexual agendas*, by L. Segal. New York: New York University Press.

Shakeshaft, Carol, and Audrey Cohan. 1994. *In loco parentis: Sexual abuse of students in schools: What administrators should know.* (ERIC Document Reproduction Service No. Ed 372 511).

Shamgar-Handelman, Lea. 1994. To whom does childhood belong? In *Childhood matters: Social theory, practice and politics*, edited by J. Qvortrup, M. Bardy, G. Sgritta, and H. Wintersberger. Hong Kong: Avebury.

Sibley, David. 1995. Geographies of exclusion: Society and difference in the West. New York: Routledge.

Silin, Jonathan. 1994. *What can we know? Advocating for young children.* Paper presented at the American Educational Research Association Meeting. New Orleans, LA.

———. 1997. The pervert in the classroom. In *Making a place for pleasure in early childhood education*, edited by J. Tobin. New Haven: Yale University Press.

Skibinski, Gregory. J. 1995. The influence of the family preservation model on child sexual abuse intervention strategies: Changes in child welfare worker tasks. *Child Welfare, 124*:975–988.

Slunt, Emily T. 1994. Living the call authentically. In *Being called to care*, edited by M. E. Lashley, M. T. Neal, E. T. Slunt, L. M. Berman, and F. H. Hultgren. Albany: State University of New York Press.

Sorenson, Gail P. 1991. Sexual abuse in schools: Reported court cases from 1987–1990. *Educational Administration Quarterly, 27*:460–480.

Spiegel, Lawrence D. 1988. Child abuse hysteria and the elementary school counselor. *Elementary School Guidance & Counseling, 22*:275–283.

Spodek, Bernard, O. Saracho, and M. Davis. 1991. *Foundations of early childhood education: Teaching three, four, and five-year-old children.* Upper Saddle River, NJ: Prentice-Hall.

Spodek, Bernard, and Olivia Saracho. 1994. *Right from the start: Teaching children ages three to eight.* Boston: Allyn & Bacon.

Stainton Rogers, Rex, and Wendy Stainton Rogers. 1992. *Stories of childhood: Shifting agendas of child concern.* Toronto: University of Toronto Press.

Steinberg, Shirley R., and Joe L. Kincheloe. 1997. *Kinderculture: The corporate construction of childhood.* Boulder: Westview Press.

Stephens, Sharon. 1993. Children at risk: Constructing social problems and policies. *Childhood, 1*:246–251.

Stoler, Ann L. 1996. *Race and the education of desire.* London: Duke University Press.

Strickland, Jim, and Stuart Reynolds. 1988. The new untouchables: Risk management of child abuse in child care—before establishing procedures. *Child Care Information Exchange, 63*:19–21.

Taeuber, Cynthia M. 1991. *Statistical handbook on women in America.* Phoenix: Oryx Press.

Terzian, Phillip. 1997. Child care dilemma: The trouble with the Woodward case. *The Honolulu Advertiser,* 5 November.

Tharinger, Deborah, J. Krivacska, M. Laye-McDonough, L. Jamison, G. Vincent, and A. D. Hedlund. 1988. Prevention of child sexual abuse: An analysis of issues, educational programs, and research findings. *School Psychology Review, 17*:614–634.

Thompson, Audrey. 1998. Not the color purple: Black feminist lessons for educational caring. *Harvard Educational Review, 68*:522–554.

Threadgold, Terry. 1990. Introduction to *Feminine, masculine and representation,* by T. Threadgold and A. Cranny-Francis. Sydney: Allen & Unwin.

Tiefer, Leonore. 1995. *Sex is not a natural act and other essays.* Boulder: Westview Press.

Tobin, Joe. 1997. Playing doctor in two cultures: The United States and Ireland. In *Making a place for pleasure in early childhood education,* edited by J. Tobin. New Haven: Yale University Press.

Todd, Sharon, ed. 1997. *Learning desire: Perspectives on pedagogy, culture, and the unsaid.* New York: Routledge.

Too, Yun Lee. 1995. *The rhetoric of identity in Isocrates: Text, power, pedagogy.* New York: Cambridge University Press.

Touch Research Institute. 1997. Homepage. Available from http://www.miami.edu/touch-research/ (12 November 1997).

Trickett, Penelope K., and Elizabeth J. Susman. 1988. Parental perceptions of child-rearing practices in physically abusive and nonabusive families. *Developmental Psychology, 24*:270–276.

Turner, John, and Nick Sparrow. 1997. Hearing the silence: The spiral of silence, parties and the media. *Media, Culture & Society, 19*:121–131.

United States Bureau of the Census. 1991. *Statistical abstract of the United States* (113th Edition). Washington, DC.

United States Department of Health and Human Services—National Center on Child Abuse and Neglect. 1996. *Child maltreatment 1994: Reports from the state to the National Center on Child Abuse and Neglect.* Washington, DC: GPO.

Valverde, Mariana. 1987. *Sex, power and pleasure.* Philadelphia: New Society Publishers.

Vance, Carol. 1984. Pleasure and danger: Toward a politics of sexuality. In *Pleasure and danger: Exploring female sexuality,* edited by C. Vance. Boston: Routledge & Kegan Paul.

Wagener, Judith R. 1998. The construction of the body through sex education discourse practices. In *Foucault's challenge: Discourse, knowledge, and power in education,* edited by T. Popkewitz and M. Brennan. New York: Teachers College Press.

Walkerdine, Valerie. 1984. Developmental psychology and the child-centred pedagogy: The insertion of Piaget into early education. In *Changing the subject: Psychology, social regulation and subjectivity*, edited by J. Henriques, W. Hollway, C. Urwin, C. Venn, and V. Walkerdine. London: Methuen.

Watney, Simon. 1987. *Policing desire: Pornography, AIDS and the media*. (1st Edition). Minneapolis: University of Minnesota Press.

Weeks, Jeffrey, and Janet Holland. 1996. *Sexual cultures: Communities, values and intimacy*. New York: St. Martin's Press.

Wells, Stephen, N. Davis, K. Dennis, R. Chipman, C. Sandt, and M. Liss. 1995. *Effective screening of child care and youth service workers*. Washington, DC: American Bar Association Center on Children and the Law.

Wilczynski, Ania. 1997. *Child homicide*. London: Oxford University Press.

Witz, Anne, S. Halford, and M. Savage. 1996. Organized bodies: Gender, sexuality and embodiment in contemporary organizations. In *Sexualizing the social: Power and the organization of sexuality*, edited by L. Adkins and V. Merchant. New York: St. Martin's Press.

Zavala, Iris M. 1992. A gaze of one's own: Narrativizing the Carribean. (An essay on critical fiction). In *Feminist Critical Negotiations*, edited by A. Parker and E. A. Meese. Philadelphia: John Benjamins Publishing Company.

Index

A

abusive practices, x
"activist" critique, "no touch" policy,
 89
Adams, Phillip, xii–xiii
administrator, on "no touch" policy,
 42
AIDS
 awareness, need for, 70
 moral panic issue, 19
American Association for Protecting
 Children, 28
American Association of University
 Women, molestation survey,
 29
Angelou, Maya, 62
Appelbaum, David, 10
attachment bonds, 7, 13
authenticity, of touch, 10

B

background checks, day care workers,
 32, 63
"bad touch," distinguishing, 31, 63
*Behaviors of Preschoolers and Their
 Teachers*, 65
Ben-Yehuda, Nachman, 25
Bennett, Peter, 22
"best practice," pedagogy, xi
Bowlby, John 7
boys, special needs of, 67
Bredbeck, Gregory W., 89
Breiner, Sandra J., 24

Buckey, Ray, 20–21
Buentipo, Ruebyne, 24–25
building trust, 13
Bulger, James, 17–18

C

caregiver-patient relationship, 11
caregivers
 description of, 8
 marked identities of, 84–85
 self-inquiry of, 81
 surveillance of, 45–47, 75, 76,
 80, 83
caring relationship, nature of, xi
Carter, Kathy, 88
"case history with holes," 37
child abuse
 American response to, 20
 in Canada, 26
 false reports of, 29
 in the family, 30
 fear of charge of, 14, 20
 historical reality of, 24, 27
 injuries from, 25
 media stories about, 20–21, 23–
 24, 26, 27
 problem of, 28, 29
 reconstruction of, 27
 in schools, 27–30, 75
child-adult relationship, regulation of,
 ix, 22–23, 32–33
child care
 invention of, xii

touching practices in, 9, 10
"Child Care and Mobile Children's
     Services Regulations," 32
child-child relationship, regulation of,
     ix
child development, x–xi
     pedagogical practices, 10
child killing, practice of, 24
child protection legislation, ix–x
child-rearing practices, contradictions
     in, xiii–iv
"child savers," 22
child sexual abuse, ix, 3, 28, 29, 75, 85
     interventions against, 30
childhood sexuality
     discussion of, xiii, 64–67
     normative discourse, 68–70
children
     impact of "no touch", 77–79, 85
     modern construct of, 19, 23, 70
     problem students, 18
     violence among, 18
"Cleveland affair," 86
Clinton, Bill, 63
Cohan, Audrey, 28–29
Cohen, Stanley, 4, 19
Connell, Robert W., 67
corporal punishment, disallowance of,
     28
Crossentower, Cynthia, 93
cultural resources, stories, 37
"cultural scripts," 71
curricula, child abuse prevention, 30,
     85

D

Davies, Bronwyn, 12
"Day Care Center Goes to Extreme to
     Protect Reputation," NPR,
     37, 53, 91–95
day care center, "no touch" policy, 2–5
"Day Care on the Net," NPR, 83
deconstructions, definition of, 15
Del Prete, Toni, 32
DeMitchell, Todd, 29
Department of Health and Human
     Services Report, child
     abuse, 30

desire, of teachers, 51–53
diaper changing policies, 5, 14, 28,
     32–33, 63, 80, 81, 85
Dilg, Mary A., 36
Discipline and Punish, 45
Dittman, Laura L., 8
"dole scroungers," 20
Dowsett, Gary W., 67
Duggan, Lisa, 71
"duty of care," 11, 77, 78, 79

E

early childhood education
     confronting "no touch" policy, 71–
     72
     sexuality issues in, 62, 68
early childhood professionals
     moral panic of, 3, 21–22, 86
     touching practices, 9
ECENET, electronic server, 37
Edwards, Bob, 91
emotional support, 74
empowerment, for preschool children,
     31–32
eros
     concept of, xi, 68
     in teaching, 53
Etaugh, Claire, 66

F

family
     role of sexuality, 63
     site of child abuse, 30
fathers, behavior of, 35
Fells Acres day care center, 86
Felman, Shoshana, 86, 88
Field, Tiffany, 58, 59, 77, 93–94
fingerprinting, day care workers, 32,
     63
Flood, Mary F., 85
"football hold," 3
Fossey, Richard, 29
Foucault, Michel, 14, 15, 45
*Foundations of Early Childhood
     Education: Teaching
     Three, Four, and Five-Year-
     Old Children*, 65
Fry, Stephen, xiii

G

gender, early childhood professionals, 43–44, 48–49
gender role development, early childhood education, 67
Gilbert, Neil, 31–32
Gilligan, Carol, 81
"good touch," distinguishing, 31, 63
Goode, Erich, 25
Governing the Soul, 23–24
"green flag" touch, 31
grid of power and knowledge, 15
Grumet, Madeleine, xiii

H

Halford, S., 48
Hall, Stuart, 4, 17, 26
Harlow, Harry F., 7
Hawaii Teacher Standards Board, 10
Heller, Sharon, 13
Hendrick, Joanne, 64–66
Holland, Janet, 63
homosexuality, moral panic issue, 19
hooks, bell, 52–53
hugs
    in caregiving, 8
    forbidding of, 2, 85

I

identity, role of sexuality, 5, 63
I Know Why the Caged Bird Sings, ban on, 62
infants, benefits of touch, 8, 13
interpretive community," 36
Introduction to Early Childhood Education, 64

J

James Bulger case, 17–18
Jenkins, Philip, 20, 33
Jenks, Chris, xii, 23
Johnson, Richard, x, xiii

K

Kanka, Megan, 26–27
Katz, David, 11
Kennell, John H., 7
KIDSPHERE, electronic server, 37

Klass, Polly, 26
Klaus, Marshall, 7

L

lap-sitting
    forbidding of, 5, 81, 85
    practice of, 8
Leavitt, Robyn L., 81
Lively, Edwin, 66
Lively, Virginia, 66
Lynch, Thomas, 94

M

male caregivers
    abdication of role, 80
    diaper changing policy, 80, 85
    employment changes, 85
    marked identity of, 84–85
male teachers
    diaper changing policy, 33, 63, 85
    fear of abuse accusations, 38–43
    moral panic of, 3
    perception of, 87
    self-policing of, 45–47
massage therapy
    for children, 8, 77
    for infants, 58–59, 77
masturbation, early childhood education, 64, 67, 69
Mayden, Bronwyn, 30
Mazur, Sally, 10
McMartin Preschool case, 20–21
McRobbie, Angela, 20
McWilliam, Erica, 57, 89
media, role of, 18, 19, 22, 26, 27
medical discourse, moral panic, 85–86
Megan's Law, 27
Melton, Gary B., 85
men
    characterization as sexual perverts, 63
    in early childhood education, 49, 85
Millet, Kate, 70
Moab is My Washpot, xiii
moral panic
    characteristics of, 25

in child care, 20, 21–22, 84–85
cost of, 29
description of, 19
issues, 19–20
media spread of, 18, 19, 21, 22,
    26
medical discourse, 85–86
naming of, 33
sexual abuse 3–5, 11–12
social control mechanism, 17, 25–
    26, 84, 86–87
"moving out of silence" stories, 88–
    89

N

"Nanny Vision," 83
narratives, function of, 35–36
National Association for the Educa-
    tion of Young Children
    (NAEYC), 68
National Educational Association
    (NEA), 59
National Public Radio (NPR)
    "Day Care on the Net," 83
    day care program, 37, 91–95
    responses to day care program, 53
Nelson, Cary, 84
neonate, experience of, 13
"New Untouchables, The: Risk
    Management of Child Abuse
    in Child Care," 20
"no touch" discourse, 14–16
"no touch" narratives, xii, xiii, 35–49,
    51–52, 53–56
"no touch" policy, xii, xiii–xiv, 3–5,
    12, 14
    confronting, 55–56, 57–59, 71–
        72
    critique of, 89
    Upper Falls Children's Center, 92–
        93
Nowesnick, Mary, 20
nurture behavior
    description of, 4
    lack of, 5
    of teachers, 10–11, 13

O

O'Loughlin, Michael, 81
"oppositional discourses," "no touch"
    policy, 16

P

Paedophile Index, Australia, 35, 62
paedophilia, fear of charge of, 1
Panopticon, 45
parents, on "no touch" policy," 39–
    40, 44
pedagogic practice
    "no touch" policy, 47–48
    sensory-rich, 8
pedagogic relationship, nature of, xi
pedophiles, punishment of, ix–x
Pekor, Carrie, 10
Phelan, Peggy, 45
physical assistance, 74–75
physiological facts, early childhood
    education, 67
Plummer, Ken, 36, 67–68
politics, 5
    role of sexuality, 63
politics of vulnerability, x
Postmodern Child, The, xii
power, role of sexuality, 5, 63
Power Rangers, ban on, 18
Pratt, John, 45
Prevette, Jonathan, 2
professional caregivers, x
protection
    of children, 23–24
    of the family, 70–71
"Pure" critique, "no touch" policy, 89
Purkiss, Dianne, 59

R

Rathus, Spencer A., 66
"red flag" touch, 31
"regimes of truth," 86
responsive care, 79–81
*Rethinking Sex: Social Theory and
    Sexuality Research*, 67
Rhedding-Jones, Jeanette, 15
Rose, Nikolas, 23–24, 46–47

S

safe sex practices, 70–71

same sex marriage, moral panic issue, 19

saturation, of images, 75–76

Savage, M., 48

Scafidi, Frank A., 8

schools

    guidelines for touching in, 32, 75

    site of child abuse, 28–30, 75, 85

Secret Scars, 93

self-esteem, invention of, xii

self-inquiry, of caregivers, 81

self-policing behavior, 45–47

sex role development, early childhood education, 64, 67

sexual abuse prevention programs, 30–32, 85

sexual ignorance, 70–71

Sexual Development of Young Children, 66

sexuality

    contemporary concern about, 5, 62–63

    in early childhood education field, 63–72

Shakeshaft, Carol, 28

silence, on childhood sexuality, 70–71

Slunt, Emily T., 11, 78

Smith, Tovia, 91–95

social control, 4, 84

social control mechanisms, 17, 25–26, 86

"society of spectacle," 75

Sorenson, Gail P., 28,

Spitz, René, 7

Stephens, Sharon, 87

stories, use of, 36, 37

student teaching, tips for, 1–2

subjectivity, shaping of, 12

surveillance

    omnipresence of, 75–76

    practice of, ix, 4, 27–28, 45–47, 83–84

Susman, Elizabeth J., 30

T–U

Tanner, Joan, 92, 94

"teach, don't touch", NEA, 59

teachers

    confronting "no touch" policy, 55–56, 57–58, 88–89

    modern role of, 57

    politics of vulnerability, x

    professional standards of, 10

    reconstructing subjectivity of, 41–42

    role in child abuse, 27–29

    security measures for, 32

teaching, Socratic ideal of, 56–57

television violence, moral panic issue, 19

Tharinger, Deborah, 30

Thompson, Audrey, 35

Thorton, Sarah L., 20

Time for Kids, ban on sexual material, 63

Tobin, Joe, x, 15, 16

Too, Yun Lee, 56–57

Total Learning: Developmental Curriculum for the Young Child, 64–65

touch

    benefits of, 8, 89, 94–95. See *also* massage therapy

    interpenetrability of, 10

    role of, 11, 54–55

    teachers' practice of, 53–54

    theoretical importance of, 7–8, 12–13

    theory and practice, 56–57

touch therapy, research on, 58–59

Touch Research Institute (TRI), 5, 58–59, 77, 88–89, 93

touching, guidelines for, 32

Trickett, Penelope K., 30

"truth effect," xii, xiii

Upper Falls Children's Center, 92

V

Vance, Carol, 71

video cameras, in child care, 5, 46, 83

visualization
  of touch, 74–75
  "no touch" policy, 5, 73–74
vulnerability, social production of, x

W–Y

"Watch Me" video camera, 83
Watney, Simon, 87
Weekly Reader, ban on sexual
    material, 63
Weeks, Jeffrey, 63
Wells, Stephen, 28

*Whole Child, The: Developmental
    Education for the Early
    Years*, 64, 65–66
Wiggans, G., 81
Wilczynski, Ania, 24
Witz, Anne, 48
women, in early childhood education,
    48–49
Woodward, Louise, 26, 27, 84
work, role of sexuality, 63
World of Children, The, 66
Young Children, sexual discourse in, 68

ERUPTIONS
New Thinking across the Disciplines

Erica McWilliam
General Editor

This is a series of red-hot women's writing after the "isms." It focuses on new cultural assemblages that are emerging from the de-formation, breakout, ebullience, and discomfort of postmodern feminism. The series brings together a post-foundational generation of women's writing that, while still respectful of the idea of situated knowledge, does not rely on neat disciplinary distinctions and stable political coalitions. This writing transcends some of the more awkward textual performances of a first generation of "feminism-meets-postmodernism" scholarship. It has come to terms with its own body of knowledge as shifty, inflammatory, and ungovernable.

The aim of the series is to make this cutting edge thinking more readily available to undergraduate and postgraduate students, researchers and new academics, and professional bodies and practitioners. Thus, we seek contributions from writers whose unruly scholastic projects are expressed in texts that are accessible and seductive to a wider academic readership.

Proposals and/or manuscripts are invited from the domains of: "post" humanities, human movement studies, sexualities, media studies, literary criticism, information technologies, history of ideas, performing arts, gay and lesbian studies, cultural studies, post-colonial studies, pedagogics, social psychology, and the philosophy of science. We are particularly interested in publishing research and scholarship with international appeal from Australia, New Zealand, and the United Kingdom.

For further information about the series and for the submission of manuscripts, please contact:

Erica McWilliam
Faculty of Education
Queensland University of Technology
Victoria Park Rd., Kelvin Grove Q 4059
Australia

To order other books in this series, please contact our Customer Service Department at:

(800) 770-LANG (within the U.S.)
(212) 647-7706 (outside the U.S.)
(212) 647-7707 FAX
or browse online by series at:
www.peterlang.com